Fixing the Engine of Justice

Diagnosis and Repair of Our Jury System

David Tunno

iUniverse, Inc.
Bloomington

Fixing the Engine of Justice
Diagnosis and Repair of Our Jury System

iUniverse books may be ordered through booksellers or by contacting:

iUniverse
1663 Liberty Drive
Bloomington, IN 47403
www.iuniverse.com
1-800-Authors (1-800-288-4677)

Because of the dynamic nature of the Internet, any web addresses or links contained in this book may have changed since publication and may no longer be valid. The views expressed in this work are solely those of the author and do not necessarily reflect the views of the publisher, and the publisher hereby disclaims any responsibility for them.

Any people depicted in stock imagery provided by Thinkstock are models, and such images are being used for illustrative purposes only.

Certain stock imagery © Thinkstock.

ISBN: 978-1-4759-3237-9 (sc)
ISBN: 978-1-4759-3238-6 (hc)
ISBN: 978-1-4759-3239-3 (e)

Library of Congress Control Number: 2012910257

Printed in the United States of America

iUniverse rev. date: 1/22/2013

To my granddaughter,
Olivia James Lawrence,
born this year

I consider trial by jury as the only anchor ever yet imagined by man, by which a government can be held to the principles of its constitution.
Thomas Jefferson

I'm no idealist to believe firmly in the integrity of our courts and in the jury system—that is no ideal to me, it is a living, working reality. Gentlemen, a court is no better than each man of you sitting before me on this jury. A court is only as sound as its jury, and a jury is only as sound as the men who make it up.
Harper Lee

We have a criminal jury system which is superior to any in the world; and its efficiency is only marred by the difficulty of finding twelve men every day who don't know anything and can't read.
Mark Twain

Contents

Opening Statement

"I CONSIDER TRIAL BY jury as the only anchor ever yet imagined by man, by which a government can be held to the principles of its constitution."[1] When Thomas Jefferson wrote those words, he was summarizing his view of the importance of our jury system. What was true at the birth of our nation is true today.

Engines didn't exist then, but anchors did. And where an anchor is a fine analogy for something that prevents the drifting of a boat or the toppling of a structure, an engine keeps something moving, working, and useful. Anchors are usually simple one-piece structures that function by a factor of their unchanging and overwhelming mass. They are maintenance free. Neglect is not an issue. But an engine must be maintained and even upgraded, if necessary, to continue to meet the demands placed on it. A single faulty component can cause it to be unreliable, inefficient, or inoperative altogether. I believe this to be true of the jury system as well.

Jefferson's quote also reflects the pressing issue of his day, the formation of a new government with a constitution that represented a radical departure from the oppressive British regime. Government at the time was to be feared, and while a healthy fear of government will always be, well, healthy, perhaps today Jefferson would agree with the appropriateness of adding society, the other side of that coin, as an entity that must be held to the principles of the Constitution,

1 www.searchquotes.com

in part by means of the jury system. That is the thrust of this book, the inspiration for which came to me at 10:00 a.m. on October 3, 1995, with the words "not guilty."

It has been many years since O. J. Simpson walked free from a downtown Los Angeles courtroom, but that case still reminds us of our short attention spans. Why did we follow that trial so closely? For many, it was the best reality show ever produced—pure entertainment for those whom treachery and violence thrill. For others, it was a chance to see if the justice system would serve as well for a wealthy celebrity as for the common man. For the former group, the verdict was a bonus feature, a surprise ending that only a screenwriter could have envisioned. For the latter, it was a shock to the system, the demolition of the fundamental principle of right and wrong. "Good will always triumph over evil." Gone. "You reap what you sow." Gone. "Justice is blind." Gone.

In the first few weeks of the aftermath, we debated the deficiencies of the justice system over coffee:

- Why did the state make so many mistakes?
- Why couldn't the judge control the courtroom?
- Are high-priced criminal defense attorneys really that much better than prosecutors?
- After all that evidence to consider, how could the jury have come to a verdict in only a few hours?

The media had its feeding frenzy. Lawyers, judges, and trial consultants like me were asked for our analysis. Then the dust settled on both our televisions and our passions.

The case later came back to life in the form of the civil trial. This time, the jury arrived at the opposite decision, salving some of the wounds that the criminal trial left and giving rise to a flurry of excuses about our American justice system. Of the many offered over coffee or by television pundits, I was bothered most by those that, in so many words, offered, "It's the best system in the world. It works the vast majority of the time. Leave it alone." Right … leave it alone. Then along came the Casey Anthony trial, and we learn what happens when we leave it alone. The hue and cry over a suspect system started all over again.

Enter my engine analogy. You probably own a car. You probably depend on this car. For the sake of the analogy, let's say the car works most of the time. Ask yourself if you would consider such a car broken. Or if not broken, then it's at least in need of repair. Don't we expect more of our cars than that they work most of the time? Most won't even tolerate an unreliable car. If we have any doubts about it getting us from point A to point B, it goes in for repairs. That's how demanding we are of our cars, even though a broken car is, at most, an inconvenience.

Let's take the analogy a step further. Suppose the car works most of the time. Invariably, however, those occasions it doesn't work occur when you're driving at night, in the middle of nowhere, and in bad weather. In short, the car breaks down when you need it most. I say this car is definitely broken.

One might also offer the same observation of our electoral system and our voting rights. Best in the world? Leave it alone? That suggests we needn't have addressed any of the problems with the 2000 presidential election in Florida. Regardless of whom you favored in that election, I believe we can agree the events in Florida revealed flaws in the system that caught the attention of the world and led to changes.

Was the O. J. Simpson case the ultimate test of the jury system? I don't know. Were those murders any more significant than the murders you can read about every day? Definitely not, but the case was an important test, if for no other reason than the fact that everyone was watching. The system needed to work more so than at any time in recent memory.

The legal industry is just that—an industry. As with any industry, there's a good deal of inertia. As this industry is in large part a public one, inertia is an even greater factor. So, if there's going to be any action, the general public needs to be in on it, if not driving it. That's why I wrote this book with the general public in mind.

As indicated at the outset, I started this work started shortly after the Simpson criminal trial, but because of lack of time, it languished in the to-do file for years. During those years, additional experiences stemming from my trial consulting work have contributed to it as well as articles about trials and juries.

Because I rely a good deal on my experiences for the positions I take in this book, I'll digress for a moment to offer a brief summary of my work in this field. I began a career in trial consulting in 1989 with the firm Litigation Sciences, Inc. At the time, it was by far the largest trial consulting firm in the country. Four years later, I left to form my own practice, Tunno & Associates Trial Consulting. Briefly, my trial consulting practice includes conducting jury research (mock trials), consulting on case strategy, writing opening statements and closing arguments, coaching lawyers on their delivery and consulting on briefs, as well as teaching witness skills, creating demonstrative exhibits and, of course, selecting juries.

A detailed review of my practice is available on www.tunno. com, but I'll spend a moment or two on jury research projects (mock trials). These are projects that test a case in front of surrogate jurors who've been recruited to hear a summary version of a case and decide what would be their verdict if they were sitting as jurors in the real trial. These projects are a mainstay of the trial consulting business. They give our clients an accurate read on the strengths and weakness of their case. They are commonplace in high-profile cases and where a lot of money is at stake. You may have even participated in one.

Lawyer clients want to know, for example:

- Am I making my points effectively?
- Do the jurors hate the client?
- Is there a piece of evidence the jurors view as more important than I do?

They also want to know what profiles of jurors would be predisposed against them in the real trial, just to name a few factors.

During the jury selection phase of the trial, we typically sit at the table with the lawyers with a notepad, writing brief notes on each juror as he or she answers questions from the judge and attorneys.

We give the juror a rating number so the attorney will know who we think are the best and worst jurors for our side. Then we play the game of second-guessing the other side while we use our available strikes to eliminate the jurors we don't like.

Trial consultants come from various walks of life, but the two most common are social science researchers and those in the communications field. My expertise was in communications, and I added the social science research skills while I was in the business. For others, it might be the other way around.

To the extent the jury system was a key factor in the outcome of the Simpson criminal case, a greater tragedy is the brevity of our collective attention span. If the result of the Simpson civil trial represents some measure of correction of a previous injustice, in no way was it a vindication of the jury system itself. The results of a few trials will not correct what ails the system. If your mechanic told you last year that your transmission was about to fail and now he says you need new brakes, you still have a transmission problem. And cases like Simpson and Anthony are the ones we talk about because the media covers them so extensively. For every one of those high-profile cases, there are thousands of others. Some are small in terms of the number of people directly affected, but others affect a great many people, even huge segments of the population. These are cases few people even know about. From an insider's point of view, the system doesn't work any better in those cases than it does in the famous ones.

Ailments in our jury system represent future problems, future injustices waiting to happen. The cure is not waiting and watching. The cure is not forgetfulness. The cure won't happen by looking for signs of health. If it's going to happen, it will come by our focusing on the system's weaknesses and attacking its problems.

Part I

Problems
Before we talk about remedies, let's look at the signs of
weakness in our jury system. Here are the problem areas:
representation; competency; bias; misconduct; and nullification.

CHAPTER I

Representation

IF YOU BELIEVE THE myth that juries are representative of their communities, I urge you to observe the jury selection process in nearly any courtroom in this country. Before you take your field trip, think of the diversity of your community. Think of the tremendous variety of occupations, experiences, and skills. Having created this immensely diverse palette in your mind's eye, don't expect to actually see it in the jury pool, much less on the jury that is ultimately selected. Why not? Because large segments of the population rarely serve as jurors. The reasons are varied, but here's the short list: No-shows, lack of support from employers, flimsy excuses for not serving, and the peremptory ax.

No-Shows

During the fiscal year that ended June 30, 2004, 2.9 million jury summonses were mailed to Los Angeles County residents to try to drum up the ten thousand jurors needed daily, but the response rate was only 41 percent, authorities said.[2]

Los Angeles residents aren't alone. According to a 2007 survey by the National Center for State Courts, 46 percent of people nationally

2   "Judge Gives Wake-Up Call," *Los Angeles Times*, April 20, 2005.

show up for jury duty.[3] That average puts some communities to shame, including Manhattan (33 percent) and Boston (24 percent), according to the same report.

Reactions by the courts varies but has included the use of law enforcement. Tulare County in California saw a whopping rate of no-shows drop from 56 to 33 percent with the help of warning letters from the court and visits by sheriff's deputies. The court enlisted the sheriff's department in Lee County in North Carolina in an even more active role, as one woman experienced when she came out of a grocery store to find a deputy stuffing a summons through her car window. He then warned her, "Be there, or you'll be in contempt."[4]

Sometimes prospective jurors don't show up because they ignore the summons, a mandate from the court to show up. Maybe they know the system is overloaded and the chances are slim of the courts catching up to them. But at the same time, it is not uncommon to hear jurors describe multiple jury experiences. By the time they reach middle age, these individuals have served four, five, and six times on juries. These numbers are for actual service on a jury, not just those additional times when the individuals may have answered a summons but were never actually selected to serve on a case. Gavin Jones, an emergency room nurse in Ventura County, California, received five summonses in five years,[5] yet there are many who, even by middle age, have never been summoned.

How can there be so many people with multiple jury experiences when others have none or have never even been summoned? Is there a crack in the system into which many of our identities have slipped, allowing some to fall out of view of those in charge of summoning potential jurors? Could an A-list of jurors exist, and could getting on that list mean you're going to be called again and again? Is it like

---

3   "Getting Out of Jury Duty is a National Pastime," CNN.com, July 27, 2007.

4   "Getting Out of Jury Duty is a National Pastime," CNN.com, July 27, 2007.

5   Cynthia Overweg, "Long Wait Often Goes Along with Summons," *Ventura County Star*, April 12, 2009.

buying something online, where doing so assures you receive a flood of unsolicited online offers in the future? Why are we reticent to respond to junk mail? Because we fear the junk mail advertisers will then know our address is a good one and we are prone to responding, resulting in a mailbox full of junk mail every day thereafter. Do the courts act similarly? The facts suggest so.

Lack of Support from Employers

The hardship excuse then decimates the pool representing the relatively small percent who respond to the summonses, with financial hardship being the most common. For those who've never received and answered a summons, here's a brief explanation of how the system works. When you're called into a courtroom, you'll be one of dozens of other jurors in your pool. The judge conducts the first round of questioning in the *voir dire* process.

Voir dire, French for "to speak the truth," usually refers to the examination by the court or attorneys of prospective jurors to:

- determine their qualification for jury service
- determine if cause exists to challenge (excuse) a particular juror
- provide information about the jurors so the parties can exercise their statutory peremptory challenges (object to particular jurors without the need to state a cause)[6]

In some federal courts, this is frequently the only voir dire because federal judges often don't allow the attorneys to ask questions of their own, while in other courts, both federal and state, the judge will allow attorneys to conduct their own voir dire following that of the judge. Written jury questionnaires are sometimes used at the judge's discretion, but this procedure is relatively rare. If it is used, the court writes the questionnaires, usually with input from the attorneys on both sides, who will also have a chance to review the completed questionnaires prior to jury selection. The jurors' answers

---

6   Steven Gifis, *Barron's Law Dictionary*, 4th edition (New York: Barron's Educational Series, Inc., 1966), 545.

to the written questions are often the source of attorneys' oral voir dire questions.

The first step in the voir dire process is determining which jurors should be excused for cause. Although the judge ultimately makes the decision, attorneys usually have input into this process, with the exception of the financial hardship excuse.

Some prospective jurors simply can't afford to serve. This is not surprising, considering a few bucks a day and free lunch just isn't what they used to be, say, during the depths of the Great Depression. For example, during the writing of this book, the so-called Washington DC sniper case came to trial. Reportedly, out of a pool of 123 prospective jurors, over one-third expressed concerns that serving on the six-week trial would cause them to suffer personal or financial hardship. At the end of the first day of jury selection, the judge had excused fifty-one.[7] As it turns out, even that outcome was comparatively good.

Financial hardships are almost always due to the policy of an employer who pays for only limited jury service, typically ten days or less, and many pay nothing. It's the rare person who can take time away from work for almost no compensation. Nevertheless, there is a cure, which we'll visit later.

The ability to serve with severe financial hardship is usually the subject of the first question that the judge asks of the jury pool, and it almost always causes hands to shoot up throughout the group. Judge Henry Walsh of the Ventura County (California) Superior Court provided some odds: "Sometimes you get 20 percent return on a jury panel, and that can be a good day," even though, as Judge Walsh explains, the financial hardship factor shouldn't have the effect of eliminating so many jurors, as "Most trials last only two to four days."[8]

For lengthy trials, however, the financial hardship factor kicks in to an even higher degree. The Robert Blake case in Los Angeles

---

7   Stephen Braun, "Jury Selection Begins in First Sniper Trial," *Los Angeles Times*, October 15, 2003, A13.

8   Cynthia Overweg, "We Can't Pay for Jury Service," *Ventura County Star*, April 12, 2009, A1.

is one example. As the *Los Angeles Times* reported in November of 2004, "Jury selection in the case began last month, when more than 1,000 jurors were called to the Van Nuys courthouse for preliminary screening. Most were excused because they could not afford to be away from their jobs for the two to four months the trial is expected to last." The story went on to say that this was the second time that hundreds of jurors were summoned for that case.[9] The chief factor is the lack of support from employers.

Most people don't work for large companies, and the lack of financial support for the jury system from small employers is understandable. Rainbow Bridge Natural Foods, a sixty-employee store in Ojai, California, may be a typical example. "We pay sick leave and vacation days and provide health insurance," said co-owner Ernest Niglio. "Jury pay is just not high on my list."[10]

What about large companies? As Ventura County (California) Superior Court Judge Kevin McGee puts it, "Businesses use the legal system when they get involved in disputes, but if they're not willing to support it when it's needed for others, it's not a very appropriate approach to take."[11]

In one of my jury selection assignments, I witnessed what I thought at the time was the worst example of nonsupport by an employer I had ever seen. When questioning a prospective juror for hardship, the judge was told the employer didn't pay for jury service. He wasn't talking about a limited pay period. This employer allegedly paid nothing. Zero. The judge excused the juror.[12]

Now, you might expect, as I did initially, that the man worked for a very small enterprise. It would be reasonable to expect a very small company would find it financially burdensome to lose the

9   Jean Guccione, "Attorneys in Blake Trial Question Potential Jurors," *Los Angeles Times*, November 16, 2004, B3.

10   Cynthia Overweg, "We Can't Pay for Jury Service," *Ventura County Star*, April 12, 2009, A1.

11   Ibid.

12   The judge, unless he or she knows otherwise, takes the juror's word on the question of employer pay policies. There is no verification process, nor would there be time for one during voir dire.

production of even one employee while still having to pay that person his full salary. If you agree with me on that point, you might be as amazed as I was to learn the man worked for Bechtel, an international giant in engineering and construction.

After the jury was seated, I called Bechtel. I went as high as I could in the personnel department. I had psyched myself up to give the highest executive I could find a piece of my mind, and I was eventually transferred to someone who knew the score. But I never got the chance to chew on anyone. Not only did I discover the juror was wrong, I learned the company's jury service policy was exemplary. Bechtel's policy at the time of my call was to put no limit on the length of jury service for which they would continue to pay their employees. I complimented them. Kudos also to Costco. The retailer and employer of one hundred and forty thousand worldwide pays up to forty hours a week for the duration of a trial, no matter the length.[13] I don't know why or how the prospective juror erred about his employer's policy. He may have made an honest mistake, or he may just have wanted to avoid jury duty.

I also don't know how many companies like Bechtel are out there, but I do know there are far too few. From comments made by jurors during voir dire, my understanding has been that, for private-sector companies who pay anything, the typical period of pay is ten days. These include companies we all know as household names. That's only a two-week trial if the individual is seated as a juror on his first day of service. Many courts hold jurors for ten days, during which time they are shuffled from one courtroom to another in a pool until they are either seated or their ten days have ended.

If the employer of one of these jurors only pays for ten days, that juror can claim financial hardship if he's not seated on a case during his first day of service, as well as if the trial is expected to last longer than ten days. I usually work on major civil litigation involving disputes between large corporations. These trials frequently run much longer than two weeks. Some extend to a few months.

---

13   Cynthia Overweg, "We Can't Pay for Jury Service," *Ventura County Star*, April 12, 2009, A1.

The irony in this situation is that these companies that don't pay or pay for short periods only include many that are often involved in lawsuits themselves, as McGee of Ventura pointed out above. When this happens, I'm sure their attorneys want those juries to be selected from the most qualified people available. I'm sure they would rather not have most of the population, including some of the best-educated and successful members of society, excluded from possible service. This segment of our population, often through the actions of its employers, has abdicated a tremendous amount of power and responsibility. Recruits who aren't always up to the task fill that void.

It makes me wonder. When the executives of those companies see the results of their own litigation experiences, including verdicts they feel are unjust, do they reflect on their own policies? When they sit around their conference tables and talk about current events, such as a high-profile trial with a verdict they can't fathom, or a civil case with a damage award out of this world, do they put two and two together? Or do they instead keep their heads in the sand, believing supporting the judicial system is someone else's job?

Perhaps the perfect example of a company executive who viewed jury service as someone else's responsibility arose during the writing of this book. According to published stories, Jennifer Sutton, an executive assistant in Dallas, was looking forward to her first time serving on a jury. She had kept her employer, Affiliated Computer Services (ACS), and her boss, Senior Vice President Warren Edwards, informed of her starting day, but Edwards nonetheless gave her an assignment the night before her jury duty was to start.

Sutton went to work early the next day to complete the assignment, intending then to head for the courthouse. Instead, she was told to stay. She was in tears, pleading with Edwards, who, according to Sutton, fired her. Company executives confirmed the action but said it had been a mistake.

Edwards may have learned just how big a mistake it was when Sutton showed up for jury duty in District Judge John Marshall's courtroom and told His Honor the story. I love this next part. The judge issued a bench warrant for Edward's arrest because firing

7

employees for jury service is against the law in Texas. Deputies showed up at Edwards's office, took him into custody, and brought him before the judge. A quick apology by ACS may have saved Edwards, who was not charged, but Sutton did not get her job back. She had to sue her former employer.

Again, fast action by ACS cut short what was shaping up to be something of a PR nightmare. The same day the Sutton lawsuit made the news, the company issued a press release announcing a settlement with its former employee.[14] That fact denied us the opportunity to see what kind of jury would have sat in judgment of ACS. Would it be exactly the kind of jury discussed above, the kind that would slap ACS with a verdict completely out of proportion to the harm? If so, it would have been difficult to sympathize with them.

Affiliated Computer Services, Inc., is a Fortune 500 company. Large companies get involved in large, lengthy trials. In those trials, such companies often rely on the justice system for compensation in the hundreds of millions of dollars. Yet, here is one that, through the actions of one of its vice presidents, showed its disdain for that same system. I wanted to learn if this was the rule or an aberration.

The list of Fortune 500 companies isn't hard to get; nevertheless, for a few of them, the corporate headquarters were hard to find, so my survey ended up short of the full five hundred. I call the list the "Fortunate 474." The human resources departments of the Fortunate 474 were surveyed regarding their company's jury service policy. There were six choices: no time; up to ten days; up to fifteen days; up to twenty days; limited but over twenty days; and no limit. One hundred and sixty-five companies responded to the survey. The following chart graphs the results from those respondents:

14 "Worker Fired for Going on Jury Duty," *Associated Press*, February 8, 1999; "Woman fired for jury duty, boss in court," *Reuters*, February 8, 1999; "ACS Settles Jury Duty Lawsuit," *PR Newswire*, February 8, 1999.

The Fortunate 474

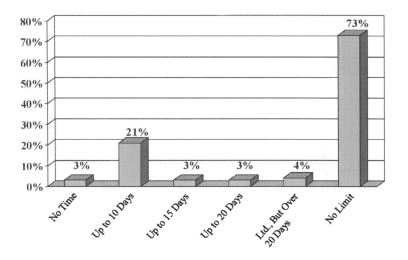

This was not a scientific survey. It relied on the willingness of someone in each of the human resources departments to respond and to do so accurately. In the case of many, it was obvious to me the request had been bounced around the company, possibly looking for someone in a position of authority to check the appropriate box. In that process, it's possible that decisions were made to not reveal company policies. My suspicion is, if responses had been received from all 474 companies, the results would have shown higher percentages in the columns to the left, reflecting policies that companies would be less proud to share with the world.

Those suspicions were reinforced when, a few years later, the results of a similar survey taken by the jury services division of the Los Angeles County Superior Court in 2001 revealed quite different results that I don't believe can be accounted for by locale or time frame. The court's survey, which I believe businesses would be much more inclined to respond to, regardless of the answers, showed the proportion of employers in Los Angeles County who pay for an unlimited period of jury service was only 22 percent, having fallen from 27 percent over the previous six years. In that same period, companies paying nothing increased from 2.3 to 13.5 percent.[15]

Of interest to me, as I went back over the above reference, I saw its mention of the economy of that year in connection with the issue: "Those in the business community say employers have become less willing to pay for jury service because of pressures to lower costs, *especially as the economy has slowed.*"[16] I italicized those last words because, compared to this moment in time (2012), references to poor economic conditions in 2001 are almost laughable. Imagine what effect that is having on employers with respect to their willingness and ability to pay for jury service now.

Nevertheless, I was pleasantly surprised to see the high percentage of responses in the "no limit" category. Those companies either have good reason to be proud of their policies or at least know what a jury pay policy should be for a good corporate citizen, especially if that corporation is a large one.

So much for the Fortunate 474. Most Americans who work for an employer don't work for these companies. If they aren't self-employed, they work for the many thousands of smaller businesses spread across the country.

There are two primary methods of sizing a company: gross revenue and number of employees. I chose number of employees to identify what I've named the "Less Fortunate 541." These are companies with twenty to forty-nine employees. I sampled them from all fifty states, more or less weighted according to population. The number 541 refers to the number of surveys sent.

According to the database I used, at that time, some sixty-seven thousand companies were in this category alone, with tens of thousands more in other employee-level categories. The companies on my list included everything from restaurants to research laboratories, floral shops to foundries, and everything in between. The list reads like a recipe for American pie. Here are the results from the 189 respondents:

15   Caitlin Liu, "Many Pay for Doing Civic Duty," *Los Angeles Times*, July 18, 2001, B1.

16   Ibid.

The Less Fortunate 541

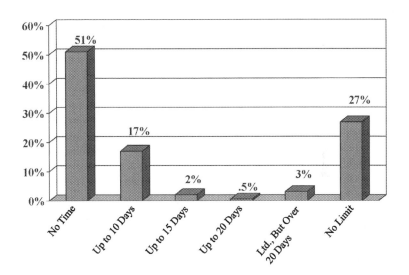

Comparing the two bar charts, you can see they are nearly mirror images of one another. That makes sense. Big companies can more easily afford to pay employees while they are on jury duty and feel less impact from the loss of an individual employee. But what is the potential impact from those companies who don't pay for jury service? Let's look at only the slice of small companies I surveyed. We'll use thirty-five as the average number of employees per company (in the category of twenty to forty-nine employees).

Remembering that there are approximately sixty-seven thousand companies in that group, let's also assume that the 51 percent in the "no time" category represents the entire population of companies of that size nationwide. That means we're looking at well over one million employees who are effectively shut out of the process from only that one very small segment of the total workforce. That is more than a million people from just that one category of employment whose views, perspectives, and knowledge will probably never benefit a jury. If you add in all of the other companies of various sizes nationwide, you can imagine how many more millions, perhaps tens of millions, are effectively excluded from the jury system. Then combine those numbers with the growing number of self-employed in this country who, in some jurisdictions, rate an automatic exclusion from jury service.

You will see in a later section of this book that the Constitution, or at least the way the Supreme Court has interpreted it over the last few decades, calls for juries to be made up from pools of prospective jurors ("venire") that represent a cross section of the community from which they're drawn. We have to ask ourselves how this is possible when support for that service is absent for many millions of Americans. Of course, identifying the problem is not enough. We must be looking for a solution.

Flimsy Excuses

Norm Crosby, the comedian, once said, "When you go into court, you are putting your fate into the hands of twelve people who weren't smart enough to get out of jury duty."[17] Norm Crosby is a comedian from the *Laugh-In* generation that many younger readers won't remember, but his cynicism on this issue isn't entirely misplaced, and I would change "smart enough" to "determined enough."

Following the test for financial hardship, the jury pool is further thinned when the judge invites jurors to offer other reasons why they cannot or should not serve on a jury. This process is usually completed in open court, so everyone can hear what excuses result in dismissal by the judge. For jurors who don't want to serve, this is a terrific way to learn the best excuses. That's not to say it's all that difficult. If you take my advice and observe a jury selection, you might be amazed at how easy it is. I've seen prospective jurors excused for reasons that astonished me.

Consider the example of an executive for a large corporation who was in a Ventura County, California, jury pool. When I say large, I mean a huge international corporation, a food giant with a well-recognized name. His reason for wanting to be excused was that he was working on a big deal. He claimed his corporation would suffer severely if he had to spend two weeks, the actual length of the trial, as a juror. Couldn't anyone fill in for him for that brief period

---

17   Brainyquote.com, December 13, 2011.

of time? Was he the only one at that multinational corporation who could do what he did? Couldn't he accomplish anything in the evenings after trial? For that matter, as an executive for a big company, wouldn't he pretty much always be working on a big deal? Isn't that part of an executive's job description? If so, does this mean he should never have to serve as a juror?

Let's see if we can lock this down. No executive should ever have to serve as a juror because he or she is always working on big deals that only he or she can make happen. Even a two-week period of partial unavailability of said individuals would be financially ruinous to their employers. This would mean that Fortune 500 companies would collapse left and right every time an executive gets the flu.

Even the juror in question seemed amazed. He sheepishly offered the court his "big deal" story. As a reasonably good judge of nonverbal communication, it was obvious to me that he didn't believe in his own cause. I think he was as stunned as I to hear it had worked, but the fact it did caused many jurors who hadn't initially offered any reason for being dismissed to raise their hands for another chance. The judge proceeded to excuse so many from the first pool of jurors (about fifty) that a second batch had to be brought in to finally seat a jury of twelve.

In the same courthouse some years later, the experience of one of my neighbors bears mentioning. He was in a pool of jurors he claimed numbered two hundred. This was the total recruit for the courthouse to fill jury seats in a number of cases starting on that day. All two hundred were questioned for one trial, but none were seated. That's none. Zero.

My all-time favorite example comes from a civil case in a Northern California federal court. The setup for this one includes the judge giving a stirring, patriotic speech prior to voir dire. I've included it below:

> I can tell you that I've talked to enough people who get summoned to jury service, and the universal reaction is, "Oh my God! I don't want to do it! Let me get out of this any way I can." And I talk to the jurors at the end of the

case, after the case is over, and they tell me universally, "That was the most interesting, educational experience I've ever had." It was like having a vacation from work and being involved and learning about something new and different, and you've become a person who is of great service to our nation. Now, I realize that this is an inconvenience. I'm not, you know, naïve about it. Many of you are involved with work and family things, and it's an inconvenient thing to be summoned to jury service, but only citizens of the United States can sit as trial jurors. It is a privilege and a responsibility of citizenship. The framers of our Constitution thought that jury service was so important and decisions of cases by jurors was so important that they wrote it into the Constitution. It's a Sixth Amendment right to have cases decided by jurors. You know why? Because you represent sort of an extension of democracy. Our whole government is based on this, people participating in government. Well, this court is a part of the judicial branch of government. How do we get people to participate in it? The jury. You represent the community, and so whenever questions of fact, that is, some dispute between parties that is something is right or wrong, whether the traffic light was green or red, those are questions or fact. And the founders of our country thought it was very important that ordinary citizens make that decision, not leaving it up to judges. There are things that I can do, but I cannot find the facts. That's for you as citizens to do. That's a very important principle of our government. And whenever we refuse to participate, we're doing something that does violence to those democratic principles. I'm sure you have watched, as I have, with the awakening of Eastern Europe to democracy—the dismantling of the Soviet Union—and they're starting to have elections in those countries. People have been thirsty to participate in their government. They've been denied the right to sit as jurors or to vote. They're thirsty to vote. We have elections in our country, [and] people won't bother to vote. If they register to vote, they don't go out to vote. We have local elections, and 17 percent of the registered voters vote. That's a small minority of the participants. If we're going to lose our freedoms and liberties and democracy, it won't be because we're invaded by any country. It's because, as citizens, when we receive a summons to participate in government, we say we don't want it. We don't want democracy. We want to live our own lives and let someone else do it. And that will be the downfall when more people refuse to participate that people say, "Look, it's inconvenient I know, but I'm willing to do it." And I urge all of you to take seriously your responsibility as citizens to step forward and serve.[18]

Makes you want to slap your hand to your heart, doesn't it? I learned later, from the court reporter who sent me the transcript, that this is the judge's standard speech. Impressive.

After the judge completed his voir dire, he invited the attorneys to ask questions, which they did before exercising their peremptory challenges.[19] That left us with a jury of eight ready to be sworn in, or so we thought. At that point, His Honor interrupted the process by asking one final question. Following is the transcript of that portion of the proceeding:

Judge: All right. Now, before I let the others go, I want to make sure that you're all delighted with your appointment to be jurors in this case, that you're anxious to serve. But I started out this case saying who wants to be the juror, you would be the ones raising your hands, jumping up and down so that we would notice you because there are lots of people who are disappointed that they're not sitting

18 *Mitsubishi Kasei Corp. v. Virgil Hedgecoth*, US District Court, Northern District of California, San Jose Division, 5/23/1996, case # C-95-20800-JW, 9–11.

19 Peremptory challenges allow attorneys from both sides to strike jurors for reasons of their own, usually without having to offer an explanation.

in those seats[20] … And I've often had the case where I've finished selecting the jury and someone says, "I forgot to tell you that it's really a problem for me." So, I want to know now if any of you have any reason why you wish to not serve as jurors in this case?[21] Excellent. Whoops![22] I knew I should have waited.

Allow me to interrupt His Honor for a moment. Why did the judge ask the question? Everyone with a hardship should have already declared it. Real hardships occur to people really quickly. So now he sees a hand raised. See if you can detect the level of urgency in the woman's words:

Prospective Juror: Well, it's kind of—I just realized my daughter just returned from college. And she's looking for employment, and we only have one car. And if she does get a job, it would be a problem, you know, with transportation.[23]

Judge: All right. What did she graduate in?[24]

Prospective Juror: Pardon me?[25]

Judge: Where did she graduate from?[26]

---

20 I'm not sure how serious the judge is, but the real question is why he is concerned that they be delighted or anxious to serve.

21 No hands were raised.

22 He saw a hand.

23 There's no urgency. She's just running this thing up the flagpole because the judge gave her the opening.

24 Who cares?

25 Even the juror was taken by surprise.

26 That's going to make a difference?

Prospective Juror: She's a sophomore at Duke University, but she's looking for summer employment.[27] She has an interview tomorrow. I would really like to do this,[28] but I'm wondering, you know, especially with looking at the times.[29] And if she does get employment with having one car available, it would be ... it might be pretty difficult. She might not be able to accept the job because of ... I intended to buy a car in about a couple of weeks, an extra car so that she could take [it] back to school eventually, but—[30]

Judge: Well, now, those are the kinds of problems that come up, and you may or may not work it out. I just don't want you to accept a position as a juror and find yourself in a circumstance where that becomes a burden on you.[31]

Now, it could be she won't get a job. I hope that's not the case, but it could be she would get a job where she could drop you off and pick you up, or it could be that other transportation arrangements could be made.[32] But this is the time to indicate if you would find that prospect of being the only driver of the only car to be something that ... where you say I think I will have a hardship for that reason.[33]

---

27   So this isn't even about the big career job. She's just shopping for a summer gig.

28   Uh-huh

29   How tough can the times be if you can afford to send your kid to Duke?

30   Can you believe this? By the way, this was taking place in a major metropolitan area with an excellent public transportation system.

31   What happened to that great speech?

32   He's starting to make sense.

33   Now he flips again! What prospect was this? This wasn't even mentioned as the hardship.

Prospective Juror: It could be.

Judge: Well, it's got to be definite. It could be, I know. Do you wish to be excused?[34]

Prospective Juror: That's a tough one.[35] Yes, I guess so.[36]

In this case, a juror was excused for hardship simply because serving would have been a minor inconvenience. The examples I've cited are not aberrations. They are extremely common. Why? The fault lies entirely with the bench.

I've observed that judges often want to be pals to jurors. They want jurors to identify with them. They don't want disgruntled jurors, and they don't want to be the bad guy who forces the unhappy prospect to do his or her civic duty. The attorneys are powerless in this situation. In practice, they can't appeal to the judge to deny the individual's wish to be excused. The attorney who did so would immediately alienate the juror to his cause, not to mention the judge.

DILBERT © UFS Reprinted by Permission

---

34   Hell yes she wishes to be excused! Why else did she bring it up? The question is when wishing to be excused became a hardship.

35   Ahhh, darn!

36   *Mitsubishi Kasei Corp. v. Virgil Hedgecoth*, US District Court, Northern District of California, San Jose Division, 5/23/1996, case # C-95-20800-JW, 89–91.

Trial by Postal Worker

If you take my advice on that courthouse field trip I recommended earlier, you will probably see the results of these inadequate jury pay policies. You will likely see a jury composed largely of government workers of one kind or another. I call it "Trial by Postal Worker."[37]

Although postal workers (and for the purposes of this book, take this to mean anyone on any public payroll) make up a relatively small percentage of our society, they constitute a large percentage of the total jury population. Federal, state, county, city, and other public-sector entities provide their employees with full pay during jury service and always, in my experience, without a time limit. This is undoubtedly true in the case of Gavin Jones, the nurse mentioned earlier in this chapter, who had received his fifth summons in five years. It is definitely true of the wife of one of my editors, John Harten, who, when editing this work noted that, while he and his wife were relatively new residents to Ventura County, she, an employee of Amgen, the largest employer in the county, had already served on two juries and received a summons every year. Could it be that Amgen's policy of paying for up to ten days of jury service makes their employees a target for the court's jury recruiting office, putting Amgen in the same company as public employers? Is it fair that government entities and good companies like Amgen and Costco should shoulder a disproportionate share of the responsible of filling jury seats in American courtrooms?

After government employees and the likes of my editor's wife, the unemployed, homemakers, and retirees will largely compose the balance of the jury. Although entrepreneurs constitute an increasingly large segment of our society, they are so extremely rare on juries that I can't recall ever seeing even one. Although working professionals, including executives, are certainly a very large segment of our society, they are also relatively rare on jury panels.

If our justice system is in the business of fair play, why not consider the lack of fairness in this aspect of the jury system? Is it fair to the public employees who have to serve a disproportionate

---

37   Dear postal workers, please do not stop delivering my mail. This is not a criticism of you or your profession. Keep reading. I'm on your side.

amount of time for jury service? Is it fair to the taxpayers who foot the bill where private enterprise will not? Is it fair to the system that would benefit from a more diverse pool of jurors? Clearly the answer to all these questions is no.

Jurors Who Get the Ax

As a reminder, peremptory challenges are the next and final stage of jury selection. They allow attorneys to strike prospective jurors without explanation. The exception to this is when one side is suspected of striking jurors for reasons of race, which is not permitted.

Predictably, each side looks to strike jurors with certain profiles depending on the facts of the case and the way the attorneys have decided to present those facts. Keep in mind that the pool has already been weakened for reasons discussed earlier. Now put yourself in the position of the attorney whose case requires jurors with strong comprehension skills. The case may even require jurors who have some relevant education or experience that can serve as a foundation for additional learning during the course of the trial. You need jurors who will pay attention to details and use them in coming to an informed conclusion. You may be looking for jurors who can understand complex issues and share that understanding with fellow jurors.

In many courtrooms in this country, you would be at a distinct disadvantage. In those same cases, opposing counsel, looking to eliminate such jurors, will almost always have more than enough peremptory challenges to do the job. It's known as dumbing down the jury, and it happens frequently. In many venues, it's very easy to do, especially in venues where well-educated jurors are rare to begin with. I'll turn myself in. I've done it many times.

This dynamic can lead to cases being lost that should have and probably would have been won but for the absence of a juror or two who could have comprehended the evidence, thought logically, followed the judge's instructions, and led other jurors along in the process. It also encourages civil lawsuits by those who take advantage of this dynamic, the ease with which juries can be dumbed down. They may know they have a weak case on the merits but believe they can prevail with a jury that will ignore the details and be persuaded more, for example, by emotional factors. In criminal matters, I believe it hinders the prosecution. The prosecution has the burden to prove its case, as it should, but that proof often requires jurors to consider and therefore comprehend scientific information and to connect dots that many are not capable of doing. I deal with this dynamic further in the following chapter.

In summary, we are dealing with a system that is more exclusive than inclusive. A number of factors exclude a large percentage of our population, along with the knowledge and experiences it represents, from the process. We are left with a shrunken slice of our society, which we place in a position of great power and responsibility, but the problems don't end there.

CHAPTER 2

Competency

DILBERT © UFS Reprinted by Permission

COMPETENCY IS NOT A significant issue in every trial. In many trials, the issues are comprehensible to all jurors. The problem is that the issues in many trials have become increasingly complex, surpassing the comprehension of many jurors. If jurors don't understand information, they tend to disregard it. This has been shown to be the case in the jury research projects (mock trials) I have conducted, as well as in posttrial interviews.

Jury research projects are usually an eye-opener for the client attorney. By the time the study is conducted, the attorney has been living with the case for some time, perhaps even years. He or she knows the case intimately.

To conduct the study, the client lawyers deliver opening statements, presenting a synopsis of the case from both sides. The surrogate jurors, recruited by phone like with any marketing research project, fill out questionnaires calling for their opinions on the key issues and then convene to deliberate the case as a group.

The deliberation process is when the client attorneys get the first data on how jurors react to the case and why. The clients sit behind one-way mirrors, watching the process unfold. What stuck with the jurors? What drove their opinions? What arguments were persuasive enough to change the positions of other jurors?

It frustrates them to learn that a key fact is completely overlooked or, for that matter, how jurors simply make up facts or use their life experiences to supplant case facts. This is a phenomenon that is also discovered in posttrial interviews with jurors, so there is no reason to believe that the actual trial causes jurors to behave altogether differently than they do in research studies. If that were so, the research studies would be valueless, and over the many decades the tool has been used, quite the opposite has been proven true.

The O. J. Simpson criminal trial serves as a real-life example of this issue. Consider the strongest evidence against O. J. Simpson in either the criminal or civil cases, the DNA evidence. DNA evidence is conclusive evidence. If there was one molecule of O. J.'s blood anywhere at the crime scene that couldn't be reasonably accounted for in some other fashion, he's guilty. Game over. Period. If there was one molecule of blood from either of the victims, especially Ron Goldman, on anything owned by O. J. Simpson, he's guilty. Furhman wouldn't matter. Views of the LAPD wouldn't matter. Gloves fitting or not wouldn't matter. "Ugly ass" shoes wouldn't matter. That should have and would have been the end of the story, but not if you didn't understand the scientific significance of DNA evidence, as was the case with one Simpson juror who equated DNA evidence with blood typing. You might, as I believe he did, focus on something you could understand, such as the glove that looked as if it didn't fit, the character of Mark Furhman, or the argument that all the blood evidence was either planted or contaminated.

You might have done what most jurors do, make the job as easy as you can. You might take the simplest, easiest path to a decision. Not consciously, perhaps, but you might nevertheless take that path.

Coincidentally, the Simpson criminal case provides an interesting and revealing perspective on the issue of juror competency, not only for what happened in Los Angeles, but also because of what one of the key figures said in a subsequent and unrelated case.

You may remember the well-publicized 1998 case of Louise Woodward, the English nanny a Massachusetts jury found guilty of second-degree murder in the death of a child under her care. The lead defense attorney for Ms. Woodward was none other than Barry Scheck, also on the Simpson defense team. Scheck took the lead in presenting the defense's version of the scientific evidence, particularly the DNA evidence.

Prior to the Simpson trial, Mr. Scheck had already made a name for himself in the field of DNA evidence, specifically as a means for proving that a convicted felon could not have committed the crime. The significance of his earlier work and reputation shows that Mr. Scheck does believe in the accuracy and power of DNA evidence, or at least when it helps his clients. Summarizing his position in the Simpson case, Scheck argued that the DNA evidence was unreliable and inconclusive. In the Woodward case, his position was that it proved her innocence.

We know the outcome of the Simpson criminal case. I'm not hiding how I feel about it or what I believe was one contributing factor, namely a lack of competency on the part of the jury. Following the verdict, I don't recall Mr. Scheck or any of his teammates saying anything on the subject of competency, nor, as advocates for Simpson, would I expect it. I am heartened, however, to learn Mr. Scheck does occasionally consider juror competency an issue. Case in point: the Massachusetts jury didn't believe his version of the scientific evidence and rendered a guilty verdict against his client, Louise Woodward.

On a talk show following the verdict, Mr. Scheck discussed that jury:

Scheck: We had a grad of Harvard Law School, an electrical engineer, an actuarial who had a grad degree, and a fellow involved in construction who deals with data all the time to make decisions. I'm not talking about an issue of intelligence.[38] It's more that you wanted to get people on that jury that felt comfortable[39] making decisions based on—assessment based on scientific and technical evidence. By the luck of the draw, we lost those individuals.[40] And the night of the verdict, I said "Go talk to those alternates. I'm sure they have a different view of the case." And sure enough, that was the case. I think that the scientific evidence was not as important to [the sitting jury] in their deliberations as it should have been. The evidence before the jury is very clear that this was an old injury."[41]

Mr. Scheck went on to discuss a challenge issued by the prosecution in the Woodward case:

Scheck: It was reported that District Attorney Tom Reilly had made a statement earlier in the day that our medical defense was foolish or ridiculous. We would very much like to have independent scientists look at this evidence, talk to the scientists from both sides, because we're very confident that we would prevail in that, and serious independent people[42] ought to look at it. It's one of those cases where, really, the scientific evidence is so strong that it has to be

---

38 Of course not. That would make him sound elitist.

39 There's that word again.

40 The names of the people he is talking about weren't drawn as part of the deliberating jury, which put them on the list of alternates. Alternates don't get a vote. They stand by in case a deliberating juror has to be excused.

41 Scheck translation: The jury based its decision on personal bias or ignorance, not an objective look at the facts.

42 Scheck translation: Which the jury was not.

examined within the scientific community.[43] I don't think that is a frivolous or inappropriate suggestion.[44]

Be careful what you wish for, Mr. Scheck. It is generally regarded as fact that defense attorneys, such as you, benefit from juries with less education.

Without belaboring the Simpson case, it may be helpful to revisit Mr. Scheck's key argument there. As you may recall, the defense contended that the police planted most of the blood evidence against Simpson from the sample taken from Simpson at police headquarters.

The problem facing the defense was that several of the blood samples (that is, the blood drops at the murder scene that followed alongside the bloody footprints) had been identified prior to the taking of Simpson's blood sample. Although the defense was otherwise claiming that the police had planted Simpson's blood, they couldn't make that argument with respect to the footprint drops.

To account for the fact that DNA analysis identified the footprint drops as Simpson's, Scheck had to come up with an explanation. My version of Scheck's argument is admittedly truncated, but it goes something like this:

> At some point, the vial of blood taken from Simpson was opened. Elsewhere in the laboratory at that time were swatches of the footprint drops that had been removed from their containers.[45] Opening the vial of blood created an aerosol effect. Microscopic amounts of Simpson's blood sprayed into the air. The aerosol containing Simpson's blood, and thus his DNA, circulated in the air. Some of it landed on the swatches of the footprint drops. Like so many airborne US Army Rangers descending on an overmatched enemy, it kicked out the DNA from those samples, the now degraded and weakened DNA of the

---

43   Scheck translation: Not by incompetents who didn't buy his spin on the evidence.

44   *Cochran and Company*, Court TV, November 6, 1998.

45   Here's where the magic of Scheck's argument comes into play.

"real" murderer, and replaced it with Simpson's DNA. That explains how the footprint blood drops tested positive for Simpson's DNA.

Key to Scheck's argument was the strength of the footprint samples or, more specifically, the DNA in those samples. Because they were several hours older than the known Simpson blood sample, Scheck had to convince the jury that they had degraded to the point where the DNA in those samples was vulnerable to take over by the DNA in the fresher sample, the known Simpson blood sample. It was degraded so much, in fact, that microscopic amounts of that known sample DNA, flying invisibly through the air, was powerful enough to transform the DNA in the footprint samples to that of the known sample, Simpson's, a complete takeover, as it were, of the identity of those footprint samples.

I am of the opinion Scheck's argument was ludicrous and he knew that even as he was making it. His expertise in DNA has helped free wrongly convicted felons before the science of DNA was fully established and long accepted by the courts. Those convicts were exonerated based on DNA testing of blood, tissue, or semen samples that were decades old, as Scheck explained in the following excerpt from a PBS interview (also in 1998):

> Scheck: When you saw a case, depending whether you're a judge, a prosecutor, a defense lawyer, anyone in the system, you see a case where somebody is convicted and they drag that individual out of the courtroom and he is screaming, "I'm innocent," and you walk away sometimes saying, "I don't know, there's some doubt." Now we can go back to those cases fifteen, twenty years later and we can find out. And literally quite a few of our clients who have been exonerated in postconviction DNA testing were dragged out of the courtroom at the time of sentencing and conviction screaming, "I'm innocent, I'm innocent" and it haunted all the people involved in the case and then

we come back twenty years later with this magical black box that suddenly produces the truth.

Q: Why are we seeing more of these cases? What's going on?

Scheck: Ever since the Justice Department published its study in June of 1996 entitled "Convicted by Juries, Exonerated by Science: The Post-Conviction DNA Cases." At that time there were twenty-eight cases. Since then seven more people have been exonerated. [That is] thirty-five. And we can go back to cases that are ten, twenty, thirty years old and retest them. And as we go back through them we're going to get more and more exonerations.[46]

Apparently, degradation isn't such a big problem after all. According to Scheck, you can get perfectly valid DNA test results on a thirty-year-old sample. Indeed, scientists have retrieved DNA samples from Egyptian mummies thousands of years old.

You may have bought Scheck's argument in the Simpson case. Maybe not. The point is that the jury either bought or completely ignored the DNA evidence and, in the process, ignored the most important evidence in the case. There is no middle ground. The argument was central to Simpson's defense. If the jurors didn't buy it, the only alternative was a conviction unless they ignored it in favor of other evidence they could better understand, for example, the glove or whether they trusted Mark Fuhrman or the LAPD. Did Barry Scheck and the Simpson trial team take advantage of a dumbed-down jury? You be the judge.

Let's get back to that previous talk show interview with Mr. Scheck, the one that followed the Louise Woodward case. What an opportunity that was for a serious independent talk show host. Scheck left himself wide open for an embarrassing comparison to the Simpson criminal case. All the host had to do was point out that Scheck's own description of the Woodward case and jury could

---

46   *Frontline*, pbs.org, 1998.

have been used to describe the Simpson case and to discredit that jury. After all, wasn't the Simpson case heavy with highly technical scientific evidence? None of the Simpson jurors had technical expertise. Could it be the Simpson jury just wasn't up to the task? That might have been a timely question to ask.

A serious, independent host could have had a field day. What was this host thinking? Oops, what was I thinking? The host was none other than Scheck cohort Johnny Cochran, one of several attorneys to get his own talk show following the Simpson case. I didn't need another reason not to watch Court TV's *Cochran and Company*, but thanks anyway.

Essentially, Scheck agrees that some jurors may not be competent to interpret complex scientific evidence. His solution, at least as expressed relative to the Woodward matter, would be to take such decisions out of the hands of jurors altogether and hand them over to a panel of "serious, independent" scientists. At least, that's what we know of his opinion when he believes it would suit his side of the case.

In the second half of this book dealing with solutions to the problems, you'll see I disagree with Mr. Scheck. It's not that I believe all jurors are capable of deciding all cases. I don't. I do believe the solution lies in a system of matching juror capabilities to the requirements of cases in much the same way as companies and institutions match job applicants' capabilities to job requirements.

As an example of some of the issues addressed here, the Simpson case works because of the exposure it provided and the resulting familiarity to most Americans, but it's not an isolated incident. Most of the cases I work on contain highly complex material. They often deal with technologies such as microchips, computer software, and electronic inventions of all types, as well as chemistry and biochemistry, including DNA technology.

Typically, much of my work in such cases is directed toward developing methods for simplifying the teaching of these technologies. Even so, much of it escapes the most capable jurors, or at least the most capable of the ones who survive the dumbing-down process, and many jurors don't get any of it.

If we want to look at the root of this problem for the purposes of attributing blame, we should start with our education system. We don't support that system, which is the same as saying we don't support our children or the future of our country. We show our appreciation for teachers by paying them peanuts and expecting them to work for the love of it. We jam children into classrooms like Japanese commuters on a Tokyo subway. We graduate students who can't read the classified ads in search of the few jobs for which they're qualified. The complexity of trials is increasing, but jurors' comprehension is not. We are dumbing down the entire nation.

Most of us are familiar with Jay Leno's "Jay Walking" segment on *The Tonight Show* where Leno takes a camera and microphone to the street and asks passersby what they know about a particular subject. The topics appear to be chosen because they are something everyone should know. "Double Jeopardy" it isn't. These questions are dirt easy. In what country is the Panama Canal? Where is the Great Wall of China? How many stars are on the American flag?

Leno targets adults in the eighteen- to thirty-year-old group. These aren't actors or people recruited for their stupidity. They just happened by. Their appalling inability to answer the questions, combined with the apparent ease with which Leno is able to find ignorant people, is the source of humor for the segment. Is there a word for hilarious but frightening? These people aren't just fodder for *The Tonight Show*. They and lots more like them are also potential jurors.

We are not the best and the brightest of the industrialized nations, and we are paying the price for it in our jury system.

Mark Twain said, "We have a criminal jury system which is superior to any in the world; and its efficiency is only marred by the difficulty of finding twelve men every day who don't know anything and can't read."[47] Unfortunately, if finding twelve people who fit Twain's description is the task, it's becoming less and less difficult, a point that apparently prompted radio jocks John Kobylt and Ken Chiampou of *The John and Ken Show* on KFI-AM in Southern California to take matters into their own hands.

----

47   quoteland.com

While the 2008 corruption trial of Orange County Sheriff Michael Carona and his wife, Deborah Hoffman, was pending, the radio show hosts featured a daily segment, "Taint the Carona Jury Pool," during which they encouraged listeners to lie in order to get on the jury and then convict the defendants. They also played audio recordings implicating the defendants. Kobylt provided the reasoning: "The truth is I don't trust juries. I don't trust twelve people who aren't smart enough to get out of jury duty. We've talked to some jurors and they're insane. There's a lot of crazy people out there and many of them end up on juries."[48]

Was the Casey Anthony case an example of insane jurors? This was not a case of a hung jury, so it is improbable that all twelve were nuts, but for me, the question of competency was front and center in that not guilty outcome. I'll be brief. In posttrial interviews, we learned that a key to the jury's decision was that the prosecution could not prove with certainty the exact cause of death. My response to those jurors is this. The cause of death was homicide!

Let's put this in perspective. If you commit murder, dispose of the body, admittedly lie about it successfully enough that the body isn't discovered until after the remains have decayed beyond science's ability to accurately determine the specific cause of death, and then are fortunate enough to get these twelve people on your jury, you walk. As ridiculous as that outcome was, I can top it. Next is a case that makes the Anthony jurors look like Nobel Prize winners.

Raise your hand if you remember the 2003 trial of Robert Durst in Galveston, Texas. I thought so. Not too many hands outside of the Houston/Galveston area. Three years prior, Durst, sixty, a member of a wealthy real estate family, had fled New York when police renewed an investigation into the 1988 disappearance of his wife, Kathleen, who has never been found. He was also under suspicion for murder of a friend, Susan Berman, whom police sought in the investigation of Kathleen. Days after police notified Berman they were about to question her, she was found shot dead. That's merely the backdrop for this case.

---

48   Stuart Pfeifer and Christine Hanley, "Radio Show Tainting Jury Pool, Ex-O.C. Sheriff Says," *Los Angeles Times*, April 17, 2008, B5.

While hiding from the New York police in Houston, Durst assumed the name of a woman he once knew, disguised himself as a mute woman, and later admitted to killing his neighbor, Morris Black. Further, he admitted dismembering Black's body and throwing it in Galveston Bay, claiming he did so with the assumption that the police would not believe his story that Black had found Durst's gun, which went off as they struggled for it. As fiction authors are fond of saying, "You can't write this stuff," but as strange and improbable as the defense was, it was the jurors' rationale for their not guilty verdict that was most astounding.

"It doesn't matter if I thought he was guilty or not," said juror Chris Lovell. "I didn't want to convict this man on what I thought. I wanted to make a decision on what I knew based on the evidence."

Here's a tip, Chris. If you had the impression that Durst was guilty before the trial started, you would have had the obligation to tell that to the court and be dismissed as a result. However, if you thought he was guilty at the end of the trial, it means you came to that opinion based on the evidence and the prosecution proved its case.

Lovell continued, "One thing that influenced my decision, and the jury and I discussed this from the very beginning of this trial, the defense told us a story, and they stuck to their guns all the way through."

So, Chris, as long as the defense sticks to its story, no matter how unbelievable it might be, that's a reason for an acquittal? Got it. But wait. That doesn't square with what other jurors said.

Durst's story was too unbelievable to consider, according to juror Eldridge Darby. "Durst had holes in his story. That's why we had to separate his story out from the facts." Another juror, Robbie Claris, confirmed Darby's account. "We took Mr. Durst's story completely out of the picture. Based on the evidence, it just wasn't there." Got that? The defendant's story was so unbelievable that the jury didn't take it into consideration and set him free as a result.

I almost forgot that some of the jurors found it significant that the victim's head was never found.[49]

Clearly, juror competency is not an easy fix. Creating more competent jurors is to raise the education level of virtually all Americans. It's a great goal, but it isn't a solution we can count on or wait for. The change then has to come from the other end, the trial end, the jury selection and screening process that will be discussed in chapter six of part three, dealing with solutions to the problems.

---

49 Scott Williams, "Durst Jurors Speak Out: 'It just wasn't there.'" Galvestondailynews.com, November 12, 2003; "Tycoon Not Guilty," skynews.com, November 12, 2003; "Jurors in the Robert Durst trial talk about the verdict," abclocal.go.com/ktrk/news, November 12, 2003.

CHAPTER 3

Bias and Misconduct

BIAS AND MISCONDUCT ARE two more issues that compromise the integrity of the justice system. Like competency or the lack thereof, this is a sensitive issue, another of the forbidden fruits for conversation. While it seemed to me to play a key role in the Simpson case, it did not receive proportionate attention in the media. Though defense attorneys played the race card again and again, as Simpson attorney Shapiro later admitted, and though race was a key, if not the only ingredient in the defense's jury selection strategy, a timid media largely avoided the issue. When African Americans rioted following the Simi Valley acquittals of the police in the Rodney King case, they did so believing bias played a key role in those verdicts. They weren't the least bit timid about it. The Simpson and King cases are only two very visible examples of the issue, but bias plays a strong role in courtrooms every day, in trials no one ever hears of.

Case in point: A few years ago, I worked for a lawyer client representing a young black man in a civil suit against the Compton police. The plaintiff had been involved in a domestic spat with his live-in girlfriend, who called the police after he left the house. It had not been a polite argument, and the plaintiff was no angel. He may have been a gang member as the police suspected. He returned from his cooling-off period to find two officers from the Compton police department in his home. They had responded to his girlfriend's call and had been interviewing her. The plaintiff showed up, and the situation quickly got out of hand.

This incident happened not long after the Rodney King case. So when one of the officers began using his PR-22 baton, made famous by the King case, visions of being severely beaten allegedly came to the plaintiff's mind. The officer in question, skilled practitioner that he was, whose physical appearance suggested he was out of shape and, according to the evidence, was logging some patrol time to meet a payroll requirement, promptly lost his baton to the plaintiff. He then felt the business end of it himself before the plaintiff bolted from the house and ran down the dimly lit street. He ran as fast as he could but not fast enough to outrun the bullet that struck him in the back, paralyzing him for life from the waist down.

Because we represented the plaintiff in this case, federal court in Los Angeles was not where we would have preferred to be. The federal district draws from a broad geographic area, including many historically conservative communities. Nevertheless, we had a good case factually, and we were looking to get the defendant a damages award somewhere barely into the seven-figure range, which was certainly not out of line considering Rodney King's multimillion-dollar award, money he was able to spend standing up. Jury selection would be a key.

We used all our available strikes as well as we could, but it wasn't enough. We learned afterward that during the several days of deliberations. All but one of the mostly Caucasian jury were in favor of a plaintiff verdict and had been trying to persuade the lone holdout, a young white male from Orange County. Without a finding of liability, no damages could be awarded.

The Orange County juror refused to change his position and, according to other jurors, never stated his reasons for it. The result was a hung jury and a denial of any award to the plaintiff. Such is the system in the federal courts, which, unlike the state courts, require a unanimous verdict, even in civil cases.[50]

According to accounts from the other jurors, they were frustrated in their efforts to persuade the lone defense juror, who wouldn't explain his position. In effect, he wouldn't deliberate. I'm convinced he simply had a strong bias against the plaintiff and wasn't willing or able to put it aside. If he held a position that he believed to be valid, based on the evidence and the applicable law as the judge explained it, he would have explained that position. That is human nature, and it's also consistent with all the juror behavior I have seen in research projects. Being a lone dissenter tends to make a juror reticent to fight against the rest of the panel but not to be entirely silent.

The juror had control over his vote. Jurors don't have to explain their verdicts, and individual jurors can stick to a position during deliberations without explaining it either. That is how sacred we hold the privacy of the jury deliberation process. All this juror had to do was be patient, knowing that the judge would eventually have to declare a mistrial. He would then have had a hand in denying the plaintiff his award. That one vote may be the most power this juror will have in his life.

Biases show up for and against all races, as well as many professions, the government, the police, big businesses, and foreign companies, just to name a few. Knowing bias exists drives strategic litigation decisions.

I once got a call from a trial consultant friend of mine who was seeking an opinion. Her client, a Japanese company, was suing an American company for patent infringement. My friend wanted to know my opinion on the best venue, out of several alternatives, in which to sue.

It's called venue shopping. If you have a choice of communities, the question becomes, "Where can I get the best jury for my issues?" It's done because certain biases are known to be more prevalent in some venues than in others. Wilmington, Delaware, for example, has

---

50   A hung jury in a civil case produces a choice for the plaintiff: try the case all over again (very expensive) or attempt a settlement. In this case, an out-of-court settlement resulted in a payment to the plaintiff equaling a small fraction of what was originally sought.

been known to be friendly to plaintiffs in patent infringement suits. The same holds for Madison, Wisconsin, while the Minneapolis/ St. Paul venue is a bit tougher if you're the plaintiff in that type of case.

When trial consultants conduct mock trials and other forms of jury research, bias is one of the central issues we look for. This was the case when, in 1995, attorneys for Sheik Omar Abdel Rahman and others sought evidence to support a change of venue motion for their clients accused of plotting to blow up the UN building, the George Washington Bridge, the Hudson river tunnels, and other targets. Believing their clients could not get a fair trial in New York, the lawyers conducted surveys of public sentiment. To their surprise, New York was not shown to be clearly worse than alternative venues.[51]

Those findings were essentially replicated in 2002 when attorney Richard Lind sought support for a change of venue motion, a motion to move the trial out of Manhattan, for his client, a suspected aide to Osama bin Laden. Indeed, his surveys showed that 9/11 had personally affected 58 percent of New Yorkers, but the judge rejected the request, citing other evidence that similar sentiments existed elsewhere.[52]

The above two cases came up in connection with discussions of the proposed New York venue for the trial of Khalid Shaikh Mohammed, alleged mastermind of 9/11. Those discussions also revealed possible bias on the part of at least one expert (emphasis added). "Not all American jury pools have the *diversity and open-mindedness that New Yorkers are famous for*," said Daniel C. Richman, a Columbia law professor and former federal prosecutor in Manhattan. "I suspect *people elsewhere would probably be a whole lot quicker to close their ears to anything the defendants had to say*."[53]

Floridians may still remember the case of *People vs. William Lozano*, a case I worked on, where the outcome was different.

51   Benjamin Weiser, "Deciding Terror Trial Location Becomes a Complex Case Itself," *New York Times*, December 26, 2009, A1.

52   Ibid.

53   Ibid.

Sometimes compared to the Rodney King case, the Lozano case featured a policeman defendant who shot and killed a suspect racing at him on a motorcycle in Miami. The driver died, and his passenger was killed in the crash. Lozano is Latino, while the two on the motorcycle were both black, though the evidence showed Lozano could not have known that at the time.

Unlike the King case, which spawned riots after the criminal trial verdict, the Lozano incident itself prompted three days of rioting. The King and Lozano cases actually overlapped in time, with the results of the former probably affecting the change of venue considerations for the latter, as defense attorney Roy Black described many years later:

> How poisonous was it? The entire courthouse was cleared during jury deliberations. Two armored personnel carriers were stationed in front, snipers on the roof and men with body armor and machine guns in the stairwells. A no-fly zone. Just the type of atmosphere for a calm deliberate consideration of the evidence. Lozano was convicted of manslaughter. The sentencing hearing was carried live on local TV to satisfy the unruly mob, and Lozano was sentenced to seven years. The appellate court promptly reversed the conviction noting the atmosphere was more akin to an armed camp than the sober calm reflection needed for a trial. A new judge ordered a change of venue to Orlando, 225 miles from Miami. Finally things were looking good until disaster struck again. On April 29, 1992, the police officers in the Rodney King case were acquitted. In the ensuing riots 53 people died, thousands more were injured, with property damages of roughly $1 billion. In a knee-jerk response, our judge immediately changed the venue to Tallahassee because it had a larger population of African Americans. The reason was fairly

obvious. We challenged that several times, finally getting the trial sent back to Orlando, the bucolic home of Disney World, with the only threat coming from the Pirates of the Caribbean. After three weeks, on May 29, 1993, four and a half years after the shooting, Lozano was finally acquitted.[54]

Bias is not difficult to uncover, at least where research is concerned. For example, bias against large companies is prevalent in our society, especially in the population who tend to serve on juries. A large company being sued by a small company or an individual is at a disadvantage from the start, regardless of the facts in the case. In my experience, if that large company is also an insurance company, the bias against the defendant tends to be even greater.

Bias, however, is often difficult for jurors to admit to, making it difficult to uncover during voir dire. It's also difficult for them to set aside, no matter how strongly worded or convincingly delivered is the judge's admonition to do so. Such admonitions amount to pixie dust sprinkled over the juror's head. I have seen jurors' admissions to bias during voir dire serve only to prompt the judges to ask if they can set those biases aside. The judge will ask, "Can you be fair?" Most of us think of ourselves as fair people and will answer yes to that question, leaving the attorney for one side or the other to use up a strike (peremptory challenge) to get rid of the juror. Trusting a juror to set aside a bias against his or her client would be tantamount to legal malpractice.

Jurors with a bias frequently also have an agenda. The trial can become the vehicle, the opportunity, to exercise that agenda in a way more powerful than anything they could hope for the rest of their lives. The Orange County juror discussed earlier may be a good example of what has been termed a "stealth juror," a label attributed to a trial consultant friend of mine and former colleague, George

---

54   Roy Black, royblack.com, March 28, 2011.

Speckart, PhD, and his coauthor, another trial consultant, Edward Bodaken.[55]

Feelings of power and powerlessness are key components in a trial consultant's jury selection strategy. They are linked to a concept known as "locus of control." Individuals with an "internal locus of control" believe they are primarily in control of their own destiny. Those with an "external locus of control" believe external forces largely beyond their control regulate their destiny.[56] Whether or not it is consciously held, either belief system can have a direct impact on the predisposition of a juror.

Economic factors also play a significant role. While the economy has been very good to a small segment of our society, for the rest, living the American dream is becoming increasingly difficult. Bitterness and resentment often result, leading to a predisposition to favor the party in a lawsuit with which the juror can identify, the alleged victim. The results often take the form of surprisingly large verdict awards, such as in the McDonald's coffee spill case.[57, 58]

You may remember the case. A woman spilled McDonald's coffee in her lap. The coffee was very hot, and she suffered some degree of skin burn. This was a classic "David and Goliath" case, an individual plaintiff against a large corporate defendant. The plaintiff may have been a very sympathetic person but wouldn't necessarily have to be, nor would it be necessary for the defendant to be particularly despicable. This was not a defendant accused of polluting the earth or causing death due to carelessness. They were merely accused of making coffee too hot. A defendant's wealth alone, in cases like this, becomes a key factor against it.

Feelings of powerlessness can stem from the very fact we live in an enormous country. If one focuses on the whole of our society compared to his or her part in it, one may feel relatively powerless.

---

55   Edward M. Bodaken and George R. Speckart, "To Down a Stealth Juror, Strike First," *The National Law Journal* 19(4) (1996).

56   allpsych.com

57    $2.7 million in punitive damages

58   "The Actual Facts About the McDonald's Case," lectlaw.com, 1996.

These feelings are prevalent, notwithstanding our power to vote. The issue becomes one of relative power. For example, when we vote in a national election, we are one vote in tens of millions. Not a lot of power there. By contrast, when we vote on a jury, we are one vote in twelve (or fewer in a federal court jury). Depending on the case, that one vote can carry a tremendous wallop, making the jury experience a unique opportunity, a rare instance when one vote can have an enormous impact. It offers power to the otherwise powerless. For jurors who yearn to exercise an agenda, the temptation of that much power can be too much to resist.

Witness a civil case in Los Angeles against the LAPD. A police car struck a man while he was fleeing from officers. A jury awarded him $1.5 million for his injuries. The judge, however, overturned the verdict, citing, among other factors, juror misconduct.[59, 60]

The misconduct component stemmed from the comments of one juror, who, according to her fellow jurors, said she disliked police officers because of a parking ticket she had received. I made a follow-up call to the district attorney's office to fill in the details.

Apparently, during the course of the trial, an officer was in the process of writing the woman a ticket, but she talked him out of it, arguing it was only a quick stop. Later she returned to her car to find a ticket on the windshield, possibly, according to the assistant district attorney with whom I spoke, having been written by an officer or parking patrol person who had come along later.

The judge always instructs jurors not to consider outside influences in making their decisions, but rather only that evidence presented to them in court. Here the woman apparently considered

59 "Judge Throws out $1.5-Million Verdict," *Los Angeles Times*, November 7, 2000.

60 A judge can overturn a guilty verdict in a criminal case if he or she feels the evidence against the defendant wasn't sufficient. A not guilty verdict in a criminal case cannot be overturned. In a civil case, the judge can reverse a verdict in favor of either side. Such a decision from the bench is sometimes called a "Judgment notwithstanding the Verdict" or "Judgment *non obstante verdict* (JNOV)," which essentially means, "You jurors got it wrong. I'm a judge, and I know better."

her experience as evidence that police can't be trusted and used it in making her decision on the case at issue.

I had a similar experience with a juror in a civil case in Texas a few years ago. *Sofpool v. Intex* was a case involving two design patents on above-ground backyard-type swimming pools. We (Sofpool) showed the jury photographic evidence of the defendant's swimming pools, photos taken with the defendant's attorney present, and compared them to the patent drawings. It's standard procedure in such a case.

The jury found against us, and we were lucky enough to find out why. The jury foreperson, apparently feeling somewhat sympathetic, told us afterward that she just couldn't find in our favor because her husband works with Photoshop, which she knew to be capable of allowing the user to manipulate photographs. She arrived at that conclusion and likewise convinced the other jurors in spite of the fact that no such evidence was introduced at trial and no objections were ever lodged by the defense against our photographic evidence.[61]

Los Angeles, ever the venue for high-profile cases, experienced yet another police conduct scandal, the so-called Rampart case. For readers outside of Los Angeles, the case involved officers of an antigang unit who, among a host of other charges, allegedly fabricated evidence against gang members. Following the trial in which three of the officers were convicted, an alternate juror complained of misconduct on the panel. She alleged jurors were prejudiced against the police, joked about police witnesses, and discussed the case outside the courtroom, a violation of the judge's instructions. Other jurors reportedly complained that one person slept through much of the trial while another sulked during deliberations, reading a magazine rather than joining in the discussion.[62]

Filmmaker Michael Moore's *Capitalism: A Love Story* factored in the dismissal of a juror in a New York case against Citigroup. The juror had actually been a part of the production of the film, which was not revealed to the court during voir dire. During the trial, she

---

61   It wasn't true.

62   Twila Decker and Ann W. O'Neil, "Alternate Rampart Juror Complains of Panel's Conduct," *Los Angeles Times*, November 17, 2000, B1.

also made derisive comments about the defense within earshot of the court reporter and then lied about it to the judge.[63]

Religion also factored into a case of juror misconduct wherein jurors allegedly consulted a higher source in arriving at their conclusions. That conduct resulted in a death penalty verdict being thrown out in a Denver, Colorado, case where it was revealed that five jurors studied Bible verses during deliberations.[64]

Online and Off the Reservation

THE INTERNET AND ITS progeny have created yet another means by which jurors inclined toward misconduct can exercise that propensity, and they are running with it. Internet-related violations of judge's instructions not to communicate regarding a case outside the deliberation room and not to consult outside sources of information have led to numerous examples of juror misconduct, driving judges to distraction, wreaking havoc in courtrooms, and resulting in many mistrials.

A Reuters Legal study compiled in 2010 found that in at least ninety cases in the previous eleven years, the verdicts were subjected to challenges because of alleged Internet-related juror misconduct, and not surprisingly, more than half of those occurred in between 2008 and 2010 as Internet use increased and services such as Twitter and Facebook emerged. The article went on to cite several examples ranging from what might seem relatively minor, such as looking up the definition of "prudent," which nevertheless resulted in an overturned verdict in a manslaughter case, to:

- A juror contacting a defendant via MySpace (new trial granted)
- Another juror using the Internet to enhance his knowledge of sexual assault injuries (new trial granted)

---

63   Bob Van Voris, "Terra Firma Juror Dismissed After Citigroup Questions Movie Link," Bloomberg.com, February 11, 2010.

64   "Death Penalty Thrown Out Because of Jury's Bible Study," *Los Angeles Times*, March 29, 2005, A16.

- Another juror blogging about the trial lawyers, one of whom she thought was cute (juror dismissed)

That Seattle juror apparently saw nothing wrong with her actions, inasmuch as the judge had instructed jurors not to tweet, but made no mention of blogging, leading a public defender to comment, "We believe, probably stupidly, that jurors follow judges' instructions. They don't."[65]

According to the *Sacramento Bee*, in 2009, a San Francisco judge, in an abundance of caution, dismissed six hundred jurors because some admitted conducting online research on the case at issue. Five jurors who friended one another on Facebook during the trial led to a challenge by Baltimore Mayor Sheila Dixon of her misdemeanor embezzlement conviction. Another case in Florida was declared a mistrial after eight jurors admitted surfing the Web about their case.[66] In possibly the worst example, a judge in Fresno, California, ordered a new trial for a convicted killer after learning that the jury foreperson (the foreperson yet) brought legal documents he obtained online into the deliberation room.[67]

All the above cases and many more are causing courts to scramble to find ways to prevent such activity, from additional jury instructions to threats of fines, but the insidious nature of the activity makes it difficult to curtail. You will note that all the aforementioned examples include the fact that the jurors were either caught or admitted to the activity, a point amplified on by Greg Hurley of the National Center for State Courts in Williamsburg, Virginia: "The thing that makes the electronic media issue a little different is that it is so accessible and anonymous," he said. "Jurors

65   "As jurors go online, US trials go off track," *Reuters*, December 8, 2010.

66   Paul Elias, "Jurors on Twitter giving judges the jitters," *Sacramento Bee*, March 8, 2010, A3.

67   "Juror misconduct gets killer new trial," *The Record*, April 22, 2012, A2.

face exposure if they go to the library or drive by a crime scene, but there's little risk in going online."[68]

Jury Instructions and Burdens of Proof

In addition to the instruction from the judge to base their verdicts only on the evidence presented in court, jurors in criminal cases are also directed to decide only the guilt or innocence of the defendant. Judges do the sentencing according to guidelines. Jurors, however, routinely ignore those instructions after they become aware (often deliberately through defense attorneys or inadvertently from the media) of the possible sentence for a crime. Death penalty cases are obvious examples but not the only ones.

During one of my many revisits to this book project over the years, a high-profile case was playing out in nearby Santa Barbara. It drew attention because it involved a Superior Court judge accused on six criminal counts stemming from a domestic violence incident with her domestic partner, another woman. Of the six counts, only two were felonies, and the defendant was acquitted of one of those (threatening her partner with a gun). The jury also acquitted her of all but one of the four misdemeanor charges. She was found guilty of drunk driving.

The remaining felony charge was for disabling a phone to prevent the partner from making a 9-1-1 call. The prosecution argued she had done so to prevent the partner from making the call and thereby exposing the relationship. Conviction on either of the felonies would mean automatic rejection from the bench. In addition, the phone charge carried a maximum three-year prison sentence.

As it turns out, that possible maximum sentence was too much for one of the jurors. While his eleven colleagues voted guilty, he held out to hang the jury on that count, offering his reasoning in a posttrial interview. "It looked like the penalty was too much."[69] In

68   Paul Elias, "Jurors on Twitter giving judges the jitters," *Sacramento Bee*, March 8, 2010, A3.

69   William Overend, "Judge Found Not Guilty on Felony Count," *Los Angeles Times*, August 29, 2003, B8.

holding out for the reasons he stated, the man gave himself powers beyond that of a juror. He appointed himself judge and lawmaker.

The problem of juror bias becomes even greater and much more sinister when jurors lie in order to serve on a panel. It happens especially in high-profile cases where jurors know their vote is going to get attention, indeed when the jurors themselves are going to get attention. Witness the Simpson criminal trial and the publicity that jurors sought. Ironically, the only juror not to participate in a book deal or other publicity was the only one to be dismissed from service for allegedly planning to do just that.

The subsequent Simpson civil trial had its own bout with honesty. Jurors were replaced for not disclosing pertinent information. Juror Rosemary Caraway's decision not to disclose her daughter's employment with the district attorney's office, in response to a specific item on the written questionnaire, provided defense attorney Robert Baker with an issue he could use to support his appeal of those verdicts.

That same trial provided us with yet another example of juror bias and, had the outcome been different, possible juror misconduct. The issue arose after the trial when many of those jurors participated in a televised press conference immediately following the verdicts. The comments of one woman in particular were very enlightening.

To appreciate her remarks, we need to consider the instructions civil juries get from the judge. This one is no exception. Included in those instructions is a description of the burden of proof.

Different levels of proof are required of the party bringing a suit to trial, depending on the type of case and, with respect to some civil trials, the issues. The most widely understood is the burden on the prosecution in a criminal trial, which is described as being beyond a reasonable doubt. It means the prosecution must prove beyond a reasonable doubt that the defendant is guilty. It might be argued that some jurors don't know what is meant by "reasonable" and the court does not provide a definition, but that's another matter. Obviously, the standard is there to make certain a criminal defendant gets a fair chance. The prosecution bears a heavy burden of proof and rightly so.

On the other hand, civil trials carry a much lighter burden of proof for the plaintiff, known as a "preponderance of the evidence". Before turning a case over to the jury for deliberation, the judge will define this level of proof for the jury. Typically the explanation will include something to the effect that, "If you find that it is more likely than not that the plaintiff is right, then you should find in favor of the plaintiff." This is sometimes referred to as the 51 percent rule, meaning that, if a juror is at least 51 percent convinced the plaintiff is right, the juror should find in favor of the plaintiff.

Yet another version of the explanation asks the jurors to visualize the scales of justice in the following way.

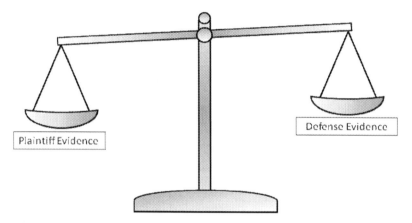

A preponderance of the evidence is the burden of proof on the plaintiff in a civil trial. It's often described as the requirement that the plaintiff tip scales of evidence at least slightly in its favor, as shown above.

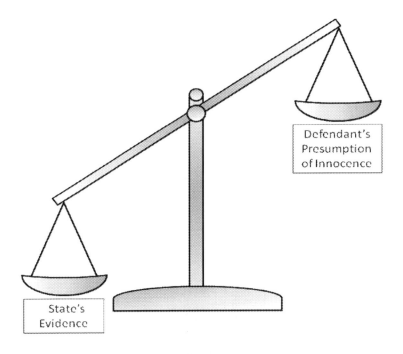

"Beyond a reasonable doubt" is the burden borne by the prosecution (the state/the plaintiff) in a criminal case to overcome what our system calls the presumption of innocence. Logically, it is the heaviest burden of proof. As an aside, this presumption is often misstated, even by those who should know better. It's probably just a bad habit, but we have all heard someone say that an accused is "innocent until proven guilty." Not so. Whether or not someone is guilty is a fact. It might be a fact known only to the defendant, but it is a fact nevertheless and quite different from a presumption of innocence. The presumption of innocence is not a fact but a state of mind the jury must adopt until they hear the evidence.

It could be that the mistaken notion that one is innocent until proven guilty has influenced the outcomes of some trials. It's hard to tell. The bigger problem is with the concept of "reasonable." What is it? How much doubt is enough to be uncertain of guilt? How much is enough to acquit? How much can still be present for a finding of guilty? It's totally within the mind of each individual juror. Frankly, the subject is probably best dealt with in a work of its own, so I'm going to leave it alone, except to say that jurors who are reasonable themselves, that is, people who can separate fact from emotion, comprehend details, follow instructions, and dedicate themselves to their duty as jurors, can best determine the notion of what is reasonable doubt. To that extent, this book does address the issue.

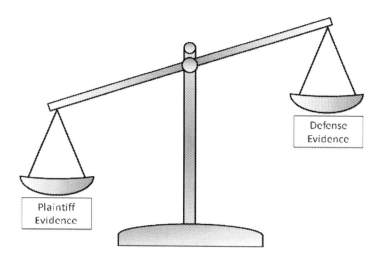

Finally, the burden of proof known as "clear and convincing evidence" is applicable to some issues in civil trials. Most jurors are never required to apply this special burden. As depicted above, it is often described as being somewhere between the previous two examples. Just as with reasonable doubt, clear and convincing elicits different notions to different people. Thank God it doesn't come up that often.

You get the idea. The important considerations here are that these are directions from the judge and it's important for jurors to understand and adhere to different levels of proof. Jurors aren't supposed to make up their own evidence or their own rules.

With that backdrop, consider this Simpson juror's remark (again, in the civil case) that, for her, it was necessary to find Simpson at fault beyond a shadow of a doubt. I believe she used the term "guilty" rather than "at fault" or "liable." "Guilty" is not an appropriate term for a civil trial, but we can understand her confusion.

Now, she did find in favor of the plaintiffs, meaning she found Simpson liable for the deaths of Nicole Brown Simpson and Ron Goldman, but clearly she ignored the standard given to her by the judge[70] and devised her own standard. And what a standard! Not only was it a higher standard than what is called for in a civil case, it was higher even than the criminal standard, beyond a reasonable doubt.

Was this a case of "no harm, no foul"? She agreed with the other jurors, so it was a unanimous decision. Okay, but what if she hadn't? What if she and two other jurors[71] had decided in favor of Mr. Simpson based on her contrived burden of proof?

Here was a juror who, probably without realizing the ramifications of what she had said, openly admitted to her own private burden of proof. How often is such a burden in play without such an admission? Here we are back to the subject of reasonable again, and I'll leave the subject with the comments I made earlier.

Jury Nullification: An Abuse of Power

This is a subject I spent considerable time both investigating and debating whether to include in this book. The argument against including it focused on the notion that, once you open that can, you play hell trying to deal with all the slippery issues inside. Indeed, having completed the book, I can verify that is exactly what happened. I felt like Alice, chasing a rabbit down a hole into an alternate reality where fact and fiction were difficult to distinguish. I also feared it was a subject that would become such a focal point as to be a distraction. Although it isn't what this book is about, it's such an important issue that I decided the book would be incomplete without a treatment of it, and I didn't want to be haunted by its omission.

---

70 The plaintiffs had to prove their case by a preponderance of the evidence.

71 The plaintiff in a civil case must persuade nine out of twelve jurors.

That said, I don't suggest my treatment is comprehensive. It's a more appropriate subject for a book in and of itself. Indeed, there are many books on the subject as well as countless articles. It's a subject I may never come to grips with completely, but having given you that somewhat windy disclaimer, I'll tell you where I stand on it now.

As defined by *Black's Law Dictionary*, "jury nullification" is the following:

> A jury's knowing and deliberate rejection of the evidence or refusal to apply the law either because the jury wants to send a message about some social issue that is larger than the case itself or because the result dictated by law is contrary to the jury's sense of justice, morality, or fairness.[72]

Advocates for nullification want jurors to vote their consciences, even if those feelings run counter to law, and to do so in spite of an oath they take to the contrary. To begin with, I question whether someone who takes an oath with the expressed purpose of violating it has a conscience.

The nullification movement argues that juries should be notified of their right to nullify the law if they disagree with it. At present, this is not the case in courtrooms, and the subject has stirred up a great deal of debate. It's also an issue that is quite old.

John Gay, English poet and dramatist (1685–1732), once said, "The jury has a right to judge both the law as well as the fact in controversy."[73] You will notice John Gay was not a legal scholar, nor was he American for that matter, but the notion of jurors as judges of the law, the essence of nullification, has found support among those who at least claim to be legal scholars and who are definitely Americans.

72   Bryan A. Garner, *Black's Law Dictionary*, 7th edition (New York: West Publishing, Co., 1999).

73   Searchquotes.com

Among those who are both legal scholars and Americans is James Joseph Duane, an associate professor at Regent Law School in Virginia Beach, Virginia. Nullification supporters, including the Fully Informed Jury Association (FIJA), maintain it is a constitutional right and support their position with the *Juror's Handbook, A Citizen's Guide to Jury Duty* and a companion piece, *Jury Nullification: The Top Secret Constitutional Right*, both by Duane.

"In a Constitutional system of justice, such as ours, there is a judicial body with more power than Congress, the President, or even the Supreme Court. Yes, the trial jury protected under our Constitution has more power than all these government officials. This is because it has the final veto power over all 'acts of the legislature' that may come to be called 'laws.'" After citing an example of what the author claims was an act of nullification, Duane continues, "That is the power of the jury at work; the power to decide the issues of law under which the defendant is charged, as well as the facts."[74]

---

74   James Duane, "Jurors Handbook, A Citizen's Guide to Jury Duty," www.caught.net, August 1, 2007.

One would think that, if a writer would reference the Constitution in support of a position, he would actually cite it. Show us the language in the original document or any of the amendments. He doesn't do that; nor can he. It isn't there, and when you read both of Duane's pieces, the actual connection between this right and the Constitution is revealed as an illusion.

His opening attempt to lay a foundation for his position begins with his assertion that the right started with the Magna Carta, which he says "created the basis for our Constitutional system of justice."[75] No, it didn't, and no, it isn't. The Magna Carta doesn't touch the issue of jurors' rights to determine the law, and a full read of it will not remind the reader much of our Constitution. Luckily for us. The Magna Carta, in this connection, is discussed further in chapter four.

Then Duane justifies his position by claiming, "At the time the Constitution was written, the definition of the term 'jury' referred to a group of citizens empowered to judge both the law and the evidence in the case before it."[76] I can't comment on that claim because I don't have a dictionary printed at the turn of the nineteenth century; however, I did find Noah Webster's 1844 edition that defines "jury" as "a number of freeholders, selected in a manner prescribed by law, empanneled and sworn to inquire into and try any manner of fact, and to declare the truth on the evidence given them in the case."[77] Other than Webster's archaic spelling of "empanneled," that definition reads as if it were written today. It says a jury decides what the facts are based on the evidence provided. No mention is made of juries also determining the law.

Later, Duane quotes Chief Justice John Jay who, in 1794, gave instructions to a jury in the first jury trial ever conducted by the Supreme Court in which he indeed gave that jury the power Duane seeks for all juries, saying, "It is presumed that juries are the

---

75   Ibid.

76   James Duane, "Jurors Handbook, A Citizen's Guide to Jury Duty," www.caught.net, August 1, 2007.

77   Noah Webster, *An American Dictionary of the English Language*, 1828. mshaffer.com.

best judges of facts. It is, on the other hand, presumed that courts are the best judges of law, but still, both objects are within your power of decision … You have a right to take it upon yourselves to judge of both [sic], and to determine the law as well as the fact in controversy."[78]

To begin with, instructions to a jury, even by a Supreme Court justice, do not a law make, much less a constitutional amendment. Justice Jay's instructions were, however, the subject of considerable debate among the Court's justices, notably in *Sparf and Hansen v. United States*, a case Duane also cited, including references to the more complete text of those instructions and inconsistencies within them.

Author Duane then continues offering support for his position by citing various appeals court decisions. It should be noted that appeals court decisions, like Justice Jay's instructions, are not the law of the land. That said, the upshot of the cases Duane cites (*US vs. Dougherty* and *US vs. Moylan*) is that the general verdict rendered by jurors gives them the inherent ability to ignore the law. They don't have to explain their verdict, so the public never knows why they reached it. Was it because they determined the facts favored one side over the other, or did they find fault with the law? I maintain that is not the same as juries having the right to determine the law. It does, however, provide jurors with the means by which to get away with doing so.

Nevertheless, the constitutions of three states—Maryland, Indiana, and Georgia—include the right of jurors to judge the law as well as the facts of a case, while the others don't. For example, the California Supreme Court in 2001 ruled that jurors must follow the law.[79]

Supporters of nullification cite examples such as the Salem witch trials in colonial America, in which jurors nullified the antiwitch laws by setting defendants free even in the face of overwhelming

---

78   James Duane, "Jurors Handbook, A Citizen's Guide to Jury Duty," www.caught.net, August 1, 2007.

79   Maua Dolan, "Justices Say Jurors May Not Vote Conscience," *Los Angeles Times*, May 8, 2001, B1.

evidence they had broken the law. Another example of the good that has come from nullification is the history of Northern juries nullifying the runaway slave laws existing prior to the Civil War. Both of these are fine examples of jurors overruling the laws of their times for the sake of justice.

FIJA wants judges to inform jurors of their right to judge the law, not only the facts. However, until judges do so, FIJA publications teach prospective jurors how to practice nullification, including how to cope with the conflict between the oath jurors take to follow the law and the act of nullifying that law, essentially how to justify violating their oath and how to get away with it. That advice includes informing those jurors that they can't be punished for their decision, regardless of their oath. FIJA literature also advises jurors to disguise nullification verdicts by attributing them to reasonable doubt so as to avoid criticism.[80]

According to FIJA, nullification sends a message regarding unjust laws. In their opinion, sending enough messages will effect changes in those laws.

Opponents label the practice as akin to sanctioning vigilantism, empowering small groups of people, or even individual jurors, to take the law into their own hands. They want jurors to decide the facts of the case, not the law. Naturally, they don't emphasize the cases cited above by FIJA. Who could find fault with those decisions? On the other hand, nullification supporters don't emphasize the many cases of white jurors in the South freeing Klan members in lynching cases. Certainly there are cases of juror nullification in those examples of American legal horror stories.

The yin and yang of this issue is that the nullification supporters have more fear of the power of government, in the form of legislators, judges, and prosecutors, than they do of individual jurors. Opponents fear individuals being empowered to exercise so much control over the laws they consider to be the cement that keeps us from dissolving into anarchy.

---

80 "Q & A, A Primer for Prospective Jurors," www.fija.com, July 24, 2003.

While I find within myself, to a degree, sympathetic with nullification supporters, on balance, I have to side with its opponents. In arriving at that position, I am not so much swayed by what opponents of nullification use to support their positions as I am by what the proponents themselves say.

In a de facto sense, juries have the power to nullify anyway in the form of a general verdict. They don't have to explain their decisions, and unlike guilty verdicts, verdicts to acquit are irreversible in America. Though this is a tremendous power, it does not make it a right, at least in the legal sense. That, I believe, is the crux of difference in the two schools of thought. Nullifiers want judges to be forced to inform juries of this right, while opponents see it as a power and therefore not an appropriate subject for jury instructions.

Nevertheless, I might find myself supporting the nullification movement if it had a focus, such as a particularly draconian law. If that were the object of its attention, I could find myself getting behind the movement with respect to a particular law after a history of debate regarding its validity, such as the debate over slavery that raged in this country for decades prior to the Civil War.

For example, if I were living in the days before the Civil War, I would certainly support the antislavery movement in any way I could. Likewise, I would try to save accused witches from burning in Salem, Massachusetts. A philosophical point of departure between me and the nullifiers is that I would hopefully be willing to pay the price for it.

Let's look at how one pays the price for these kinds of actions. Those of us who are old enough to remember the Civil Rights Movement of the fifties and sixties know what I'm talking about. Protestors broke the law by engaging in illegal demonstrations to protest segregation laws. That resulted in many thousands of people going to jail for that cause, but it worked. These demonstrators were willing to go to jail for the cause. It's a very American thing to do.

Martin Luther King Jr. seems to have agreed with that position in the following quote:

In no sense do I advocate evading or defying the law …
That would lead to anarchy. An individual who breaks
the law that his conscience tells him is unjust, and who
willingly accepts the penalty of imprisonment in order to
arouse the conscience of the community over its injustice,
is in reality expressing the highest respect for law.[81]

Paying the price for protesting an injustice is usually preceded
by more conventional methods within the system, such as voting,
voicing your opinion in the press, or participating at a public forum.
If that fails, and assuming the cause is worth it, those efforts can
be followed by participating in civil demonstrations or even civil
disobedience that carries the risk of incarceration. The civil rights
laws on our books, just to name a few, came about in this fashion,
not through jury nullification.

I don't see the advocates for nullification positioning their cause
as a last resort. Instead, it is offered as a chance to pull the trigger
on an issue under a cloak of secrecy and, further, a trigger that can
be pulled by a single gunman, not the will of the people.

That lack of consequences and avoidance of responsibility
identifies what, for me, is the insidious nature of nullification. It's
a stealth tactic. It is subterfuge, and the perpetrator needn't even
have a strong enough commitment to the cause to suffer for it.
Indeed, the cause itself needn't be important to anyone but that one
juror. It prompts the believer to take the law into his or her own
hands without a downside to that decision. In *Q&A, A Primer for
Prospective Jurors*, FIJA teaches its disciples how to nullify without
being detected:

[A] recent US Court of Appeals decision held that if
you make known your intention to acquit the defendant
regardless of the evidence against him, you may be
removed from a jury as "incapable" of being impartial.
[3] But that same decision may now protect your right
to discuss and judge the law and its application with the

---

81   quoteland.com

other jurors before deciding on a verdict: as long as you also express "reasonable doubt" that the evidence proves the prosecution's case, it cannot be established that you intended to acquit "no matter what."[82]

In November 2002, South Dakota voters rejected an attempt to make law a measure allowing defendants to argue against the law and the penalties. That is, they could do what has been done in the three states mentioned earlier. It was ultimately rejected 78 to 22 percent. A strong majority of South Dakotans showed they wanted jurors to respect the law, not put themselves above it. A *Los Angeles Times* story on that South Dakota ballot measure contained the following excerpt I found particularly relevant:

> Andrew Liepold, a law professor at the University of Illinois disagrees [with nullification]. He has studied jury nullification too. His conclusion: Just because jurors sometimes ignore the law does not mean they should be encouraged to do so. "Trials aren't designed to make policy judgments," he said. "Folks who don't like the law," he added, "should work through the process to change it." That's not good enough for Jason Koistinen, 23, a first-year law student at the University of South Dakota. "It takes too long," he said.[83]

I'll warrant that FIJA and the nullification movement in general would probably not want to be represented publicly by that first-year law student, but his position was nonetheless representative of theirs. And like a lot of twentysomething Americans, he wants gratification now. He just doesn't get it. Enacting and changing laws are supposed to take time. That time is supposed to be taken reasoning the pros and cons.

---

82   "Q & A, A Primer for Prospective Jurors," www.fija.com, July 24, 2003.

83   Steven Simon, "Is a Law Unjust? One State May Allow Juries to Decide," *Los Angeles Times*, October 30, 2002, A1.

Chapter two discusses juror competency. If you agree with me, it includes some scary examples of juror incompetence. We have to ask ourselves if we want twelve people like the ones in the Durst or Casey Anthony juries deciding what is or isn't a good law.

In the more open, public process of changing laws, state legislators and federal senators and representatives get involved. Perhaps many of them aren't much smarter than Durst or Anthony case jurors are, but at least they are people we get to vote for. Sometimes, through the initiative process, we all get to vote directly on laws. Compare those processes with the power of twelve people to make that decision with no accountability or, worse, one person.

Nullification advocates attempt to assuage concerns regarding the practice by saying it isn't relevant to civil trials because a judge in a civil trial can overturn a jury verdict and either party can appeal. While technically true, the message lacks sincerity. It ignores the fact that most judges are reluctant to reverse jury verdicts. That goes for the appeals courts as well. This position also ignores the high cost of litigation and the barrier that imposes on the parties seeking resolution from a jury in the first place.

In her book *Juror's Rights*, author and nullification advocate Jacqueline Stanley writes that nullification is not relevant to civil trials because there is no threat of jail or execution, "so it is not necessary for the jury to act as the conscience of the community."[84] Ludicrous!

The results of civil trials directly affect our lives to a much greater degree than criminal trials do. They affect our livelihoods, our cost of living, our environment, our taxes, our health, and all of our quality of life issues. Civil cases overturn laws and write new ones. Exxon Valdez was a civil case. Product liability cases, such as the Dalkon Shield, tobacco, and asbestos litigations are all civil cases, as are the numerous examples involving tires that tend to blow out, SUVs that like to roll over, shareholders suing corrupt corporate officers, and countless civil rights and antitrust cases. It is a list

---

84 Jacqueline Stanley, *Juror's Rights: Everything You Need to Know Before You Go to Jury Duty*, 2nd edition (Naperville, IL: Sphinx Publishing, 1998), 57.

almost without end. Jurors in these cases are absolutely acting as the conscience of the community.

As the definition of nullification cited earlier states, it is a "deliberate rejection of the evidence or refusal to apply the law." It is not limited to those actions taken solely to thwart the law. A deliberate rejection of the evidence also constitutes nullification regardless of the type of case and the possible remedies in civil cases.

In the Compton case described earlier, was the man from Orange County practicing jury nullification? Did he disregard the facts in favor of his own bias and agenda? Apparently, his fellow jurors thought so. Those of us who believe O. J. Simpson was guilty of murder would probably agree that nullification was a factor in that verdict as well. It is a factor in countless cases, famous and unknown, in courtrooms across America every day.

Finally, FIJA's own literature belies any claim that nullification doesn't apply to civil cases. In the same brochure cited earlier, the author writes (my emphasis added): "The whole point of having a jury system is for a group of ordinary citizens to decide upon a verdict or *damage award* independent of outside influences, including government influences."[85]

Damage awards are in the domain of civil, not criminal, trials. As an aside, FIJA is absolutely right when it says that verdicts should be "independent of outside influence." Presumably, that should include the nullification movement itself.

Elsewhere in the same publication, the author writes, "You should never feel you 'owe' it to the government or to a private plaintiff to find against the defendant."[86] The reference to "private plaintiff" obviously refers to civil cases.

The ultimate goal of the nullification movement is to change bad laws. It's a fine goal, but it seems to me the proponents are placing their faith in probably the least efficient method of achieving it. The same publication I just referred to tells the reader, "You can 'hang'

---

85   "Q & A, A Primer for Prospective Jurors," www.fija.com, July 24, 2003.

86   Ibid.

the jury with your vote if you feel it's the right thing to do ... A series of hung juries in similar kinds of cases send a valuable message to lawmakers that the public has mixed feelings about the law."[87]

How does this square with the statement, taken earlier from the same publication, that advocates the use of reasonable doubt to hide the intention to nullify? FIJA is correct that juries don't have to explain their verdicts. That applies to the positions of individual jurors as well. So how do the lawmakers referenced in the previous excerpt get this valuable message? They don't. For all the lawmakers know, those hypothetical cases were decided by jurors based on the evidence.

Jury nullification is clearly another manifestation of bias. As such, it directly conflicts with the constitutional requirement for an impartial jury. Using jury service to exercise private agendas is an abuse of power and a problem that will only get worse as our country becomes increasingly fractionalized.

In "The Illegality of Advocating for Jury Nullification," attorneys Joel Cohen and Katherine Helm wrote about an example of a nullifier recruiting jurors outside a federal courtroom in New York that got the attention of federal prosecutors. Defendant Julian Heicklen will now stand trial for distributing nullification literature outside the courtroom and doing so to people he believed to be on a jury. In part, here is what his fliers contained, according to Cohen and Helm's article:

> The judge will instruct the jury that it must uphold the law as he gives it. He will be lying. The jury must judge the law as well as the facts. (not *can*, mind you, but *must*)
>
> Juries were instituted to protect citizens from the tyranny of government. It is not the duty of the jury to uphold the law. It is the jury's duty to see that justice is done ... Once on a jury, must I use the law as given by the judge, even if I think it's a bad law, or wrongly applied?

---

87   "Q & A, A Primer for Prospective Jurors," www.fija.com, July 24, 2003.

The answer is "No." You are free to vote on the verdict according to your conscience.

From the point of view of corporate defense lawyers:

Put to the test, imagine how you would feel about Heicklen's actions if you were in the midst of a jury trial in the SDNY [Southern District of New York] courthouse right now. Imagine you are defending an insurance company in a motor vehicle accident where liability is very thin, representing a pharmaceutical firm in a questionable product liability action or advocating on behalf of one or another unpopular defendant in a complex litigation where liability hinges on the interpretation of a web of statutory schemes and changes of the law over time and requires careful vetting of evidence to properly frame the factual issues for a jury. The case has taken years of disciplined and principled legal arguments and judicial rulings to best preserve the sanctity of the jury's ability to make its decision fairly and impartially and today is the first day of deliberation. Then, right around lunchtime, some jury nullification "pamphleteer" basically tells the deliberating jurors in your case to ignore whatever law and/or legal instructions they heard and vote their "conscience" to back the "little guy" or to stick it to Corporate America ... Talk about an engraved invitation for chaos—indeed, anarchy. The freedom of self-expression is rightfully in play at the ballot box, but in the deliberation room?[88]

As an example of how this issue is, at best, unsettled, the authors quote their own appeals court decision in *US v. Thomas* (2d Cir. 1997):

A jury has no more "right" to find a "guilty" defendant "not guilty" than it has to find a "not guilty" defendant "guilty," and that the former cannot be corrected by a

---

88   Joel Cohen and Katerine A. Helm, "The Illegality of Advocating for Jury Nullification," Law.com, December 10, 2011.

court, while the latter can be, does not create a right out of the power to misapply the law. Such verdicts are lawless, a denial of due process and constitute an exercise of erroneously seized power.[89]

Consider the solid logic of that statement for a moment. In slightly more laymen's terms, if a jury has a right to judge not only the evidence (facts) but also the law, then it would indeed have the right to judge that, for example, the law is too lenient in favor of criminal defendants. Therefore, it is too restrictive against a finding of guilty and could then ignore the law with a finding of guilty. What the Second Circuit has said in the above case is that, just because there is a remedy in place for an erroneous guilty verdict, that is, the court can overturn it, whereas there is no corrective procedure for an erroneous not guilty verdict, this doesn't mean the jury has the power to render a verdict that ignores the law in the first instance. If that power existed, it would also apply to the second example. Because all would agree a jury doesn't have the constitutional right or legal right in the sense of precedence to ignore the law and find an innocent person guilty, it follows there is no right to ignore the law ever.

As I stated at the outset of this section, this book is not about jury nullification. It is primarily about getting better juries, presuming that will produce better jury decisions. Achieving that will take the steam out of the antijury movement and save a troubled system that is worth saving.

Closing out this discussion, I offer a positive story of juror conduct related to the issue of bias and nullification. Attorney Ira Salzman retained me on behalf of Stacey Koon in the third Rodney King trial. Yes, there were three. The first was the state court case in which acquittals produced riots, the second was the federal civil rights case that resulted in a split verdict among the four officer/defendants, and the third was a civil damages case. We prevailed with the jury on our case that Mr. Koon should pay no damages.

89   Joel Cohen and Katerine A. Helm, "The Illegality of Advocating for Jury Nullification," Law.com, December 10, 2011.

Few may remember the television news interview that took place outside the federal courthouse in Los Angeles following the verdicts in that third trial, and probably no one outside of Los Angeles ever saw it. A member of the jury, a middle-aged black woman who, if memory serves, was the jury foreperson, spoke of her dilemma in the deliberation room. She spoke of wanting in her heart to find monetary damages against Mr. Koon, but when she considered the evidence and the law, she decided she could not do so. For her decision, and particularly because there could presumably have been a good deal of pressure on her from the community, she deserves a great deal of praise. That's integrity. Now I have already chased that rabbit farther than I had intended. Anyone wishing to continue the chase is welcome to pick up the trail.

Again during the writing of this book, a jury rendered yet another surprising verdict, this time a military one. Was bias an issue? Perhaps your own memory of the case will help you answer that question.

While on a training flight over the Italian Alps on February 3, 1998, Marine jet pilot Captain Richard Ashby flew his plane low enough to snap a gondola cable, sending twenty tourists to their deaths. He was reportedly flying one hundred miles per hour over his limit and several hundred feet below the one thousand-foot minimum.[90]

His defense included an argument that instruments in his plane were not working properly and the terrain created an optical illusion, deceiving him as to his altitude. Also, the gondola lift was not marked on the map he was provided.[91] A year later, the jury in that military court trial not only acquitted Ashby of the most serious charge, involuntary manslaughter, but also of the relatively minor charges of dereliction of duty and destruction of property.[92]

---

90   "Americas Witnesses recall cable car disaster," *BBC Online Network*, news.bbc.co.uk, February 13, 1999.

91   Tony Clark, "Marine pilot jury in 2nd day of deliberations," *Associated Press*, March 4, 1999.

92   Steve Vogel, "Marine Pilot Acquitted in Alps Deaths," Washingtonpost. com, March 5, 1999.

Not surprisingly, the verdicts provoked outrage in Italy and around Europe. What might be less surprising is that the verdict came from a jury comprised entirely of peers of the defendant—that is, other Marine officers.

The concept of a jury of one's peers is the subject of some review in Part II of this book, a point you have now reached.

Part II

<hr/>

The Foundation for Solutions

Certainly with so many problems facing the system, no single solution would be sufficient. This isn't a case like the little Dutch boy who saved the day by plugging the leaky dike with his finger. Even if the goal were to plug holes, we would soon run out of fingers. To understand my choices of solutions, it is first important to understand the guiding principles upon which they are based: jury service as a duty not a right and the need for impartial and competent jurors.

CHAPTER 4

Jury Duty

THE CONCEPT OF A citizen's obligation shouldn't be too hard to swallow. Citizens' obligations to the state aren't unprecedented in our society or any other society for that matter. I discussed this concept at greater length earlier and will be brief here.

Part of my work as a trial consultant has always been to find analogies that may help a jury understand a technical concept or maybe just accept an argument. When I offer an analogy to a client, I try to make sure it is accurate. One of the biggest dangers with an analogy is that any weakness in it may be used quite effectively against the side offering it. That said, there does seem to be an accurate analogy to jury service that I have found very useful. You can decide whether you agree.

Mostly in times of war, men are called to military service via draft. While it's not the most popular law, I think it's fair to say the draft, for the most part, has been somewhat more popular than those who dodge it. When we think of drafting men for military service, we don't think in terms of allowing those men to fulfill their constitutional right. It's an obligation. It may or may not be rewarding, depending on your point of view, but rewards are not the issue.

Neither is there a right to serve in the military, draft or no draft. Even in times of war, this country has refused induction into the military to those whom it deemed unfit for duty. We're talking about men who wanted to serve in the military during times when the nation's security was at stake but were nonetheless denied. And we're not talking about debilitating handicaps. We're talking about flat feet and the like.

If the military can be picky about who carries a gun or even a pencil during times of war, there might be a lesson applicable to our jury system. Ask yourself whether you would feel as comfortable and secure if the military were as strong as our jury system. Yikes! And yet, don't we rely on our jury system to protect our society from within?

Impartial Juries

Black's Law Dictionary defines an "impartial jury" as "a jury that has no opinion about the case at the start of the trial and that bases its verdict on competent legal evidence."[93] Who could find fault with that? Nevertheless, I suggest it's a concept we've lost sight of. As with other lost things, sometimes it helps to retrace your steps. Enter the Constitution.

Let me introduce this topic with a disclaimer. I am not an expert on the Constitution. What I've learned has come as the result of study in this one specific area. I'm going to tell you what I've read and provide you with the same material so you can judge for yourself. If my analysis is flawed, I hope to hear about it, perhaps from one of those law professors who found a new life as a TV commentator during the Simpson trial. On the other hand, if the positions I disclose during the course of this section are correct, I would also like to hear from those same individuals as to why they didn't set the record straight during that period of intense public exposure, particularly with respect to the next topic.

---

93   Bryan A. Garner, *Black's Law Dictionary*, 7th edition (New York: West Publishing, Co., 1999).

What Is a Jury of Your Peers?

At the risk of appearing as though I've been sidetracked, stay with me for a not-so-brief visit to this subject. I believe its relevance will show itself along the way. To start, would you agree with me that, for a majority of Americans, the definition of "a jury of one's peers" means "a jury of people like the defendant"? And why not? Webster defines "peer" as "a person or thing of the same rank, value, quality, ability, and so forth; equal; specifically, an equal before the law."[94] "Peer" as in "peer group" follows from that definition and is the most common use of the word. Inserting that definition into the phrase "a jury of one's peers" has led to the above misconception, which beat reporters who don't do their homework and are more interested in sound bites than sound reporting bolster.

How many times did we witness a discussion of that concept in the media in connection with the Simpson or other high-profile cases? My memory is that the concept received considerable attention during jury selection in the Simpson criminal trial. Commentators spoke of it. Media representatives spoke of it. So-called experts spoke of it. It seemed as though it was being spoken of as a fundamental right of a defendant in a criminal trial, a perception that has become commonplace among lay people, as the quote from a prospective juror, noting the absence of blacks in the courtroom of the Michael Jackson child molestation trial in Santa Barbara, California shows. "How is this man going to get a jury of his peers?" she asked. "Just look around us. How diverse is this jury?" [95, 96]

Out of New York City comes an example of interest, in part due to the fact that all three authors of a piece of legislation requiring reports on the demographic makeup of juries in that state are not only legislators but lawyers or law school graduates. The results of the first annual report commensurate with that new law was not to

94   Michael Agnes, *Webster's New World College Dictionary*, 4th edition (New York: 1999).

95   Steve Chawkins, "Quick Pick: Jackson's Jury Chosen," *Los Angeles Times*, February 24, 2005, B1.

96   It should be noted that north Santa Barbara County, where the trial was held, is less than 3 percent black.

the authors' liking. State Assemblymen Rory Lancman and Hakeem Jeffries, along with State Senator Jeffrey Klein wrote, "Jury pools that don't look like the communities they are drawn from makes the phrase 'a jury of our peers' a hollow promise."[97]

Gentlemen, as you should have learned in law school, the promise is not only "hollow," it is nonexistent. It is one thing for erroneous statements about peers to sway the Santa Barbara County resident. She gets a pass. It's quite another matter for lawyers to be as misinformed.

It's been some years now since the Simpson trial, but I remember thinking at the time that it didn't make sense. To begin with, what factors should be considered in determining one's peers? Should former football players have judged Mr. Simpson? Is that his peer group for purposes of jury selection? Let's use me as an example. I'm a middle-aged, Caucasian male. Do we stop there? Are all middle-aged, Caucasian males my peers? Doesn't sound reasonable, does it? Let's go further. I have one adult daughter. Does that further identify my peer group? What if we add my level of education? That would narrow the field somewhat, but have we yet really identified my peer group? We could narrow it again by adding income as a factor, but I'm in a pretty broad category there.

We haven't touched on all of my life experiences, goals, philosophies, and special talents, such as they are. If I will be described as part of a group, I think some of those things are pretty important. I might even argue they are all important. If I were so inclined, couldn't I also argue that a number of identifying factors should not be included in my peer group? What about gender? Men and women are very different – no argument there. With that in mind, should women be considered my peers?

See where this is headed? Taken literally, the concept of a jury of one's peers, as it has been misinterpreted, makes no sense. It can be taken to a dangerous extreme. Keeping in mind the example of the Marine jet pilot, what does make sense is that it is a concept we should avoid in its strictest sense.

97   Celeste Katz, "New York: Your Jury May Not Look Like You," Nydailynews.com, December 9, 2011.

We want to avoid it, and we have. The nation has experienced painful lessons on this subject. Probably the most significant examples of where this concept can lead are a number of hate crimes involving the murder of blacks by whites whom all-white juries acquitted. Cases such as these have prompted changes in the laws governing jury recruiting and eligibility.

That sounds like a nice segue back to the Constitution. Those who may have thought the Constitution laid out the requirements for jury trials in great detail are going to be disappointed. I offer you exhibit A and B, Article III and Amendment VI of our Constitution:

Article III
Section 2, c. Rules respecting trials.
The trial of all crimes, except in cases of impeachment, shall be by jury; and such trial shall be held in the State where the said crimes shall have been committed; but when not committed within any State, the trial shall be at such place or places as the Congress may by law have directed.[98]

Amendment VI—Rights of Accused Persons
In all criminal prosecutions, the accused shall enjoy the right to a speedy and public trial, by *an impartial jury of the State and district wherein the crime shall have been committed*, which district shall have been previously ascertained by law, and to be informed of the nature and cause of the accusation; to be confronted with the witnesses against him; to have compulsory process for obtaining witnesses in his favor, and to have the Assistance of Counsel for his defense [my emphasis].[99]

Despite what you may have thought or heard, that's as far as the Constitution goes on the subject. In a way, the Constitution, in this

---

98   Jerome Agel and Mort Greenberg. *The US Constitution for Everyone* (New York: The Berkeley Publishing Group, 1987), 30.

99   Ibid.

matter at least, is rather like the Bible. It's possible for two people to look at the same language and come up with interpretations that differ in some respects.

Even though the Constitution does not include the term "peers" in connection with juries, it has nonetheless achieved an association in that regard, which will be discussed shortly. The problem created by that association lies in the interpretation or misinterpretation of the term in this connection. It's a little like the party game "Telephone" where something is whispered in the ear of one person, who in turn whispers it to the next and so on down the line. The last person says aloud what he or she heard, and the difference from the original message is the source of humor for the game.

I blame most of the misinterpretations on media representatives who simply don't know what it means, but also on the legal experts, consulted by those media experts, who don't correct the error. As a result, too many Americans believe it means that a defendant is entitled to a jury composed, at least in large part, of people like himself or herself. From where did this notion come, and what does case law say on this point?

To answer the question, I started with *Barron's Law Dictionary*, which provides the following definition of "jury":

> A group of people summoned and sworn to decide on the facts in issue at a trial; a jury is composed of the *peers or a cross section of the community* [my emphasis]. See *328 US 217; 407 US 493*.

Included with that definition is a definition of a so-called blue ribbon jury plus commentary on that concept:

> A jury that was chosen from prominent members of the community, such as well-educated persons or persons in positions of high responsibility, thought to be particularly well qualified to serve as jurors. These juries were used for certain highly publicized cases where ordinary citizens were thought to be too influenced to judge impartially.

Such special juries raised serious constitutional questions of the right to trial by a *jury of one's peers* selected *from* a "fair cross section of the community," *419 US 522*, and are thus no longer used [my emphasis].[100]

Barron's definition is a little confusing. In the first part, the author writes "the peers, or a cross section of the community." But because it's not likely the author meant "one or the other," he must have meant that "peers" is understood to mean "a cross section of the community."

For support, the author cites three Supreme Court decisions: *US 493 Peters v. Kiff, US 522 Taylor v. Louisiana*, and *US 217 Thiel v. Southern Pacific*. Following is a review of each, which will show Barron's is wrong.

Peters v. Kiff, 407 US 493[101]

This decision was handed down on June 22, 1972, so we're not dealing with ancient history here.

It's a case with an interesting twist about a white man convicted of burglary in Georgia in 1966. Actually, he was convicted twice in the same year, having won a new trial after the first conviction. Following his second conviction, he filed an appeal on an issue not addressed originally, that there were no blacks on either the grand jury that indicted him or the trial juries (also known as petit juries) that convicted him. Further, he contended the reason blacks were not on the jury was due to their systematic and arbitrary exclusion from the jury system in that venue (Muscogee County, Georgia). According to the appeal, these exclusionary practices were happening upstream in the jury recruiting (summoning) process.

So, his real beef was with the county's jury recruiting process that culled blacks from the ranks of potential jurors, leaving little or no chance they would ever be seated. Therefore, there would be no

---

100   Steven Gifis, *Barron's Law Dictionary*, 4th edition (New York: Barron's Educational Series, Inc., 1966).

101   "US Supreme Court, Peters v. Kiff, 407 US 493 (1972)," Findlaw.com, March 11, 1999.

chance for a "fair cross section of the community." Chance is key to understanding this case and the others.

Peters was right to appeal on the basis of the process, not the end result. Even if blacks were included in the recruiting process and were thus in the pool of potential jurors, many factors during the jury selection process, including luck of the draw, could have resulted in an all-white jury anyway.

That's about the gist of it, and six of nine justices agreed with the defendant. Even the three dissenting judges recognized the jury selection process in Muscogee was illegal, but they saw no evidence of prejudice against this particular defendant, so they felt his conviction should stand.

A side benefit to researching Supreme Court cases on the issue of peer representation on a jury was that many of the cases also had a lot to offer on related issues, including those treated separately in other sections of this book, which I will mention as they appear.

Thiel v. Southern Pacific, 328 US 217

This is a very interesting case about a man who jumped out of the window of a moving train and then sued Southern Pacific for not acting on its supposed knowledge that he was out of his normal mind. The case became a battleground for the way jurors were summoned in the Federal District Court in San Francisco. It dates back to 1946, yet it offers parallels to the case previously discussed, *Peters v. Kiff* (1972).

The plaintiff's beef with the court was that its system of summoning jurors deliberately excluded those who work for a daily wage, which it did. The testimony Thiel cited from the court clerk and the jury commissioner tells the story:

> Clerk: If I see in the directory the name of John Jones and it says he is a longshoreman, I do not put his name in, because I have found by experience that that man will not serve as a juror, and I will not get people who will qualify. The minute that a juror is called into court on a venire and says he is working for $10 a day and cannot afford to work for four (dollars a day), the Judge has never made

one of those men serve, and so in order to avoid putting names of people in who I know won't become jurors in the court, won't qualify as jurors in this court, I do leave them out ... Where I thought the designation indicated that they were day laborers, I mean they were people who were compensated solely when they were working by the day, I leave them out.[102]

The jury commissioner added that he purposely excluded "all the iron craft, bricklayers, carpenters and machinists" because, in the past, "those men came into court and offered [financial hardship] as an excuse, and the judge usually let them go."[103]

According to Thiel, with the majority opinion in the Supreme Court concurring, this was a practice that had the effect of excluding a segment of society from jury service so it was not possible to obtain a jury representing a cross section of society.

What I particularly like about this case is that both the majority and dissenting opinions have a lot to offer and are very much on point with the thrust of this book and not only for clarification of the mistaken notion of "peers," as you will see below. Following are excerpts I've chosen from both opinions, beginning with some clips from the majority opinion:

> The American tradition of trial by jury, considered in connection with either criminal or civil proceedings, necessarily contemplates an impartial jury drawn from a cross section of the community ... This does not mean, of course, that every jury must contain representatives of all economic, social, religious, racial, political and geographic groups of the community; frequently such complete representation would be impossible. But it does mean that prospective jurors shall be selected by court officials without systematic and intentional exclusion of

---

102   "US Supreme Court, Thiel v. Southern Pac. Co., 328 US 217 (1946)," Findlaw.com, March 11, 1999.

103   Ibid.

any of these groups. Recognition must be given to the fact that those eligible for jury service are to be found in every stratum of society. Jury competence is an individual rather than a group or class matter. That fact lies at the very heart of the jury system. To disregard it is to open the door to class distinctions and discriminations which are abhorrent to the democratic ideals of trial by jury … In addition, jurors must be returned from such parts of the district as the court may direct "so as to be most favorable to an impartial trial, and so as not to incur an unnecessary expense, or unduly burden the citizens of any part of the district with such service" … *And under the state [California] law, "A juror shall not be excused by a court for slight or trivial causes, or for hardship, or for inconvenience to said juror's business, but only when material injury or destruction to said juror's property or of property entrusted to said juror is threatened" … Jury service is a duty as well as a privilege of citizenship; it is a duty that cannot be shirked on a plea of inconvenience or decreased earning power* [my emphasis].[104]

I emphasized the last couple of excerpts, knowing they will sound familiar. It wasn't until I investigated this opinion that I learned the very practice of excusing jurors for frivolous causes was actually a violation of California law, specifically California Code of Civil Procedure, 201. There may be similar codes in other states.

I also want to point out the author's description of jury service as a "duty, as well as a privilege of citizenship." As I've already made clear, I agree with the duty part. The author's use of privilege isn't exactly clear. While the definition of "privilege" includes the concept of "right," it can't be construed as such in this case. It's fair to assume the author used it in the sense of honor, as in, "It's an honor to serve (one's country and so forth)." Clearly, we do not have the absolute

---

104   "US Supreme Court, Thiel v. Southern Pac. Co., 328 US 217 (1946)," Findlaw.com, March 11, 1999.

right to serve as jurors. It is, after all, called "jury duty," not "jury privilege" or "right."

From the dissenting opinion, I chose the following excerpt:

> Trial by jury presupposes a jury drawn from a pool broadly representative of the community as well as *impartial in a specific case* ... *The object is to devise a system that is fairly representative of our variegated population, exacts the obligation of citizenship to share in the administration of justice without operating too harshly upon any section of the community,* and is duly regardful of the public interest in matters outside the jury system ... The Court now deals by adjudication with one phase of an organic problem and does so by nullifying a judgment which, on the record, was wholly unaffected by difficulties inherent in *a situation that calls for comprehensive treatment, both legislative and administrative* [my emphasis].[105]

"Impartial in a specific case" is the key language. The Supreme Court cases excerpted here focus primarily on the process of drawing jurors from the population into a pool from which trial jurors are ultimately selected. They are not aimed at the final step of selecting trial jurors from that pool. That is, they are not focused on the jury that is ultimately seated but on that part of the process at least two steps removed.

The Court takes the position in these cases that the system has a better chance of assembling impartial juries absent systematic practices that exclude groups or classes of individuals comprising significant portions of the community. True enough, at least from a purely statistical point of view, but the obligation of achieving impartiality can't stop there.

We will visit this issue in much more detail later, but as a preview, keep in mind the specific language emphasized above, "impartial in a specific case." It seems to recognize that, strictly speaking, there

---

105   "US Supreme Court, Thiel v. Southern Pac. Co., 328 US 217 (1946)," Findlaw.com, March 11, 1999.

are no wholly impartial jurors. Everyone has some bias on some issue. It is the specific issues involved with a specific case where achieving impartiality is a more reasonable expectation. It is also an expectation for which our current mechanism is inadequate for reasons discussed in Part I.

The second group of italicized text from above addresses the issue raised earlier in this book under "Trial by Postal Worker":

The object is to devise a system that is fairly representative of our variegated population, exacts the obligation of citizenship to share in the administration of justice without operating too harshly upon any section of the community.

Here the Court recognizes that jury duty is a burden and it's unfair to impose that burden disproportionately on any one segment of a community, for example, public employees.

I told the postal workers that I was on their side. This case shows the Supreme Court had the same issue in mind. That opinion came out of the Court in the 1940s, but the problem is with us every bit as much now as it must have been then.

Justice Frankfurter, who authored the dissenting opinion, correctly identified the scope of the problem and the source of its solution when he called it "a situation that calls for comprehensive treatment, both legislative and administrative." He called for both changes in the jury selection laws and the administration of those laws. That's an overhaul. No quick fix, no single measure, or no fingers in the dike or minor tune-up.

Taylor v. Louisiana, 419 US 522

THIS 1975 CASE CONCERNS a man convicted of the crime of aggravated kidnapping, and an all-male jury sentenced him to death. As you may have guessed by now, it was no accident the jury was all male. At that time in Louisiana, women were excluded from jury service unless they had previously filed a written declaration expressing their desire to serve. Once again, the majority of the Supreme Court concurred with the defendant's appeal on the grounds that he was denied "a fair trial by jury of a representative segment of the community." Again, the Court cited the Sixth Amendment references to an impartial jury, a right to which the Court linked the jury selection system, specifically noting that the systematic exclusion of any group of citizens is unconstitutional.

The Court's majority opinion included some language we hadn't seen in the two previously cited cases but which actually came from an older Supreme Court ruling. I've chosen the excerpt below:

> In Brown v. Allen, 344 US 443, 474 (1953), the Court declared that "our duty to protect the federal constitutional rights of all does not mean we must or should impose on states our conception of the proper *source of jury lists*, so long as the source [419 US 522, 528] *reasonably reflects a cross-section of the population suitable in character and intelligence for that civic duty* [my emphasis]"[106]

To digress for a moment, here we have the Court declaring that a reasonable shot at a cross section is not the only goal. Suitability in character and intelligence should also be considered. It sounds like the issue of competency to me.

In this majority opinion, the Court again targets the process from which the pool of jurors is drawn. That process should not be designed to preclude the possibility of achieving a cross section, but the justices do not say the final composition of the jury must reflect that same quality.

A paragraph later, Justice White, the author of the majority opinion, continues discussing the concept of a cross section but adds a very important caveat. Once again citing a prior decision [this time Williams v. Florida, 399 US 78 (1970)], the Court writes:

> [T]he number of persons on the jury should "be large enough to promote group deliberation, free from outside attempts at intimidation, and to provide a *fair possibility* for obtaining a representative cross-section of the community."[107] [my emphasis] "Fair possibility" is an important distinction.

---

106   "US Supreme Court, Taylor v. Louisiana, 419 US 522 (1975), Findlaw. com, March 11, 1999.

107   Ibid.

As with previous decisions, the Court here recognizes that a jury representing a true cross section of a community may not be possible. Indeed, later in the opinion, that point is made more emphatically:

> It should also be emphasized that in holding that petit juries must be drawn from a source fairly representative of the community we impose no requirement that petit juries actually chosen must mirror the community and reflect the various distinctive groups in the population. *Defendants are not entitled to a jury of any particular composition* [my emphasis].[108]

The last sentence says it all. "Defendants are not entitled to a jury of any particular composition." This nails both the cross section and peer issue to boot.

Consider, for example, any major city in the nation with a population that is diverse in many ways. Also keep in mind a jury of twelve. If you divide the population only by gender and race, you will already be short of chairs. Naturally, dividing the population by only those factors would be grossly inaccurate. If the goal were to achieve a true cross section, one would have to include age categories, income brackets, occupations, religions, education, and other demographic factors.

Depending on how many ways you slice the population pie, only twelve individuals, let alone as few as six in a federal trial, could never represent a true cross section of a community. Even a fair possibility of achieving that goal would be wishful thinking, and the Court has rejected that notion outright.

The thrust of the Court's opinion in *Taylor v. Louisiana*, as in the other two cases, is simply to deter the exclusion of any group in a systematic way from the jury recruiting process and to link such a nonexclusionary system to the fundamental principles of our jury system:

---

108   Ibid.

This prophylactic vehicle is not provided if the jury pool is made up of only special segments of the population or if large, distinctive groups are excluded from the pool. Community participation in the administration of the criminal law, moreover, is not only consistent with our democratic heritage, but is also critical to public confidence in the fairness of the criminal justice system. Restricting jury service to only special groups or excluding identifiable segments playing major roles in the community cannot be squared with the constitutional concept of jury trial.[109]

While he wrote a very unflattering response to the majority opinion in *Taylor v. Louisiana*, which he likened to mysticism, the lone dissenter Justice Rehnquist also offered a point, in a backhanded way, that is entirely consistent with his colleagues:

The Court does not even purport to practice its mysticism in a consistent fashion—presumably doctors, lawyers, and other groups, whose frequent exemption from jury service is endorsed by the majority, also offer qualities as distinct and important as those at issue here.[110]

Hear! Hear! I don't know how he supported his claim that the majority endorsed the "frequent exemption from jury service" of "doctors, lawyers, and other groups," but whether they did or not, his point is well taken. As discussed in chapter 1, at one end or other of the jury selection process, significant segments of society are systematically excluded in favor of other groups. Here, Rehnquist named them.

And does it really matter where the eject button is pushed in the jury selection process? If one segment of the population is left out of the summoning process while another is summoned but seldom serves, isn't the effect the same?

---

109 "US Supreme Court, Taylor v. Louisiana, 419 US 522 (1975), Findlaw. com, March 11, 1999.

110 Ibid.

My search into Supreme Court decisions on this subject turned up another case, *Duncan v. Louisiana* [391 US 145 (1968)], which, unlike the previous references, actually incorporates the phrase "jury of his peers." The following excerpt summarizes the Court's majority opinion:

> Those who wrote our Constitution knew from history and experience that it was necessary to protect against unfounded criminal charges brought to eliminate enemies and against judges too responsive to the voice of higher authority ... Providing an accused with the right to be tried by a jury of his peers gave him an inestimable safeguard against the corrupt or overzealous prosecutor and against the compliant, biased, or eccentric judge ... Beyond this, the jury trial provisions in the Federal and State Constitutions reflect a fundamental decision about the exercise of official power—a reluctance to entrust plenary [complete, absolute] powers over life and liberty of the citizen to one judge or group of judges. Fear of unchecked power, so typical of our State and Federal Government in other respects, found expression in the criminal law in this insistence upon community participation in the determination of guilt or innocence.[111]

It doesn't take a very careful read of the above excerpt to realize the Court isn't writing about the composition of juries but about jury trials versus trials decided by judges. Indeed that was the issue in *Duncan v. Louisiana*, in which the defendant was convicted of misdemeanor battery charges without benefit of a jury. He was sentenced to sixty days and a fine of $150, where the maximum possible sentence was two years and a fine of $300.

The Louisiana Constitution required juries only in death penalty cases or where imprisonment could include hard labor. The state claimed this case was an example of a petty offense not requiring a

---

111   "US Supreme Court, Duncan v. Louisiana, 391 US 145 (1968)," Findlaw.com, December 19, 2011.

jury trial. The Court disagreed and incorporated the right to a jury trial into the Fourteenth Amendment, making this a landmark case. In the process, the Court also admitted that some petty offenses may not require a jury but did not define "petty offense," leaving that to the states. Therefore, we have judges, not juries, deciding traffic infractions.[112]

Finally on the same subject, in *Holland v. Illinois*, 493 US 474 (1990), the Court's majority opinion really nails the issue. (The parenthetical statements and emphasis are in the original.)

> The [Sixth] Amendment's requirement that the venire from which the jury is chosen represent a fair cross section of the community constitutes a means of assuring, not a <u>representative</u> jury (which the Constitution does not demand) but an <u>impartial</u> one (which it does).[113]

Here, the Court refocuses the reader on the language and intent of the Constitution to provide for impartial juries, not the broader concepts of cross sections and peers, which have crept into our vernacular. I maintain that even the use of "assuring ... an impartial (jury)" in the context of achieving a "fair cross section" is a stretch without several other measures recommended in this book. That said, it would be fair to say an impartial jury is much less likely achieved if it is not drawn from a fair cross section of the community.

---

112   "US Supreme Court, Duncan v. Louisiana, 391 US 145 (1968)," Findlaw.com, December 19, 2011.

113   "US Supreme Court, Holland v. Illinois, 493 US 474 (1990)," Justia. com, December 19, 2011.

Mr. Jenkins demanded a jury of his peers, but alas, he was a poor speller.

Magna Carta

No discussion of this issue would be complete without a visit to the Magna Carta, primarily because it is so often cited in connection with our own Constitution and the peers concept in particular. Known as "The Great Charter of English Liberty," it was signed by King John at Runnymeade on June 15, 1215.

The document dealt with many issues of that time. You will hear it cited as the source of our American right to a jury of our peers. Indeed, the Magna Carta uses the term "peers" in two sections. There is more than one translation of the original Latin, and one will see considerable differences from one to the other. In the one I used, section 29 reads:

> No freeman shall be taken or imprisoned or disseized of his free tenement or of his liberties or free customs, or outlawed or exiled or in any way ruined, nor will we go against such a man or send against him save by the lawful judgment of his peers or by the law of the land. To no-one will we send or deny of delay right or justice.[114]

It's not clear if the phrase "or by the law of the land" provides an exception to the jury requirement. Today, "or" would create that

---

114   "Magna Carta, section 29," Archives.gov, December 14, 2011.

exception, whereas "and" would not. But whether it does or not, it should be understood the authors of the document wanted to prevent the nobility from imposing its will on common Englishman, who, prior to the Magna Carta, were powerless to prevent it.

Section 29 calls for a jury system where there was previously none, one in which jurors for commoners would be commoners themselves. That's a very American-like notion, except that, at least technically speaking, we don't have a class society made up of nobility and commoners. In the eyes of the law, we're all supposed to be the same, and our Lady Justice is blind.

Not so in the minds of the authors of the Magna Carta. Nobility retained much of its stature and power. Section 14 reads in part: "Earls and barons are not to be amerced save through their peers and only in accordance with the manner of their offense."[115] "Amerced" means "punished." So English noblemen had their own peers, and only they could punish other noblemen, a very un-American concept.

Also in section 14, we find what appears to be the authors' definition of "peers," and not surprisingly, it can be linked forward to our Constitution. Section 14, which includes a general guideline for amercements, also says, in part, "and none of the aforesaid amercements is to be imposed save by the oath of honest and law-worthy men of the neighborhood."[116]

Sounds familiar? Sounds like a portion of our Sixth Amendment. "In all criminal prosecutions, the accused shall enjoy the right to a speedy and public trial, by an impartial jury of the State and district wherein the crime shall have been committed."[117]

So let's give credit to the Magna Carta for giving common Englishmen rights they didn't have previously, the right to face a jury instead of an earl or baron and some ammo for our forefathers to have against a king who came along a few centuries later named George.

---

115   "Magna Carta, section 14," Archives.gov, December 14, 2011.

116   Ibid.

117   Jerome Agel and Mort Greenberg, *The US Constitution for Everyone* (New York: The Berkeley Publishing Group, 1987), 42.

Rebels with a Cause – The Vision of Our Founders

Yet another frequently cited source for understanding the origins of our jury system are the documents preceding the American revolution. In 1765, when disputes between our colony and our English mother country were already running hot, the American Congress, while meeting in New York, wrote the Declaration of Rights. The Seventh Resolution of that document established that "trial by jury is the inherent and invaluable right of every British subject of these colonies."[118]

A few years later in 1774, the Congress at its meeting in Philadelphia wrote another Declaration of Rights. Its Fifth Resolution reads: "That the respective colonies are entitled to the common law of England, and more especially to the great and inestimable privilege of being tried by their peers of the vicinage, according to the course of that law."[119]

"Vicinage" means "vicinity," and in this context, "peers of the vicinage" means "people who live in the vicinity where a crime was committed," as opposed to where a defendant lives. For obvious reasons, that makes a whole lot more sense. So immediately, "peers" cannot mean "people who are like the defendant" because the trial could be taking place in a community far from where the defendant lives and, more importantly, far different demographically.

Yet another declaration, the much more famous Declaration of Independence, restates the previous message in the form of a complaint against the king, "for depriving us, in many cases, of the benefits of trial by jury."[120] So Congress was telling King George that Americans deserved the same rights as Englishmen in post–Magna Carta England, including the right to a trial by a jury in the sense described above. That is basically the system still in place today,

118 "Declaration of Rights," *Journal of the First Congress of the American Colonies, In Opposition to the Tyrannical Acts of the British Parliament, Held at New York, October 7, 1765*, www.constitution.org, December 14, 2011.

119 "Declaration of Rights and Grievances, October 14, 1774," Library of Congress, www.loc.gov, December 14, 2011.

120 "Declaration of Independence," www.archives.gov, December 14, 2011.

though, as Amendment IV to the Constitution shows, Americans refined the concept to include the critical element of an impartial jury.

Essentially, a jury of one's peers has nothing to do with the demographic profile of a criminal defendant but has everything to do with the demographics of the location of the alleged crime. Even then, as we know, criminal trials can be moved for the benefit of the defendant to a different venue if the court determines issues, such as pretrial publicity, might hamper the defendant's case.

That leaves the concept of an impartial jury as the heart of the law, not a jury of one's peers. It is toward that end I direct many of the recommendations that follow in Part III.

Part III

Solutions
In this section, I offer a solution for every problem
identified in Part I. Some of the solutions are in use today,
to varying degrees, others are original, and some of them,
no doubt, controversial. I look forward to the debate.

CHAPTER 5

Expanding the Jury Pool

OUR ENGINE OF JUSTICE isn't firing on all cylinders, and it's largely because we have too many people in the bleachers and not enough players. So the first order of business in reforming our jury system is to expand the jury pool, vastly improving the chances that it will represent a true cross section in every venue.

The real jury pool should consist of all those jurors who have the potential to actually serve on a jury. This has to start with the recruiting process. The courts should examine their records to determine whether their methods are capable of reaching the entire eligible population. If the system is fair and balanced, it should be rare for any citizen to receive numerous summonses in their adult lives. If the jury pool is expanded and truly representative, I also recommend dropping from the list those who have already served for a period of many years.

That exemption period should also take into account the length of jury service, as attorney Mike Rains suggested in connection with a high-profile police abuse-of-power case in Oakland, California, the longest criminal trial in Alameda County history at the time. In Rains's view, the trial exemplified why "nobody ever wants to serve on a jury. They were told the trial would last three to six months, and it took well over a year (including fifty-six days of deliberations). Anyone with contacts in Sacramento should suggest a lifetime exemption so these people never have to serve on another jury again."[121]

My proposal can be thought of as the carrot part of a carrot-and-stick approach to jury service. The stick is doing your duty. The carrot component rewards you with some breathing room before that duty comes up again.

Dealing with the No-Shows

I understand the court system is overburdened, but if we're going to expand the jury pool, there must be a downside to ignoring a summons. I also understand the claim that manpower simply doesn't exist to chase after these individuals.

However, my memory of the Vietnam-era draft years tells a somewhat different tale about the government's ability to track down no-shows. As I recall, chasing after those men who tried to ignore their draft notices was done with great efficiency. I'm reasonably certain the same can be said of other time periods when the military draft was in effect. If we can enforce military draft notices, we can enforce summons to jury service.

When you consider the problem, how difficult can this be? It doesn't require any detective work. We know who the people are. We know their names and addresses. In some venues, driver's licenses are used in the jury summoning process, so we have that information as well.

Let's also consider the social pressure factor. Who among us has not heard a friend or acquaintance brag about the clever way he or she escaped jury service? The social pressure factor is nearly zero. If, on the other hand, nearly everyone was required to serve and did so, the scofflaws would be isolated, even ostracized.

---

121   Lee Romney, John M. Glionna, and Carol Pogash, "3 Former Oakland Officers Acquitted of Some Charges," *Los Angeles Times*, October 1, 2003, B1.

If money is the issue, make it financially worthwhile or even profitable. Levy a significant fine for not answering the summons. Let those fines help pay for the system, as parking fines help pay for law enforcement. This is not a new concept, and thankfully, it's in force in some of our cities. The *Philadelphia Inquirer* reported on August 24, 2000, that up to 55 percent of Philadelphians summoned for jury service simply ignore the summons. Having had enough of that, the City of Brotherly Love was dishing out bench warrants and $250 fines in Juror Scofflaw Court.[122]

Philadelphia is not alone in cracking down on scofflaws. The *Los Angeles Times* reported in August 2002 that LA was sending out ten thousand notices a week to those who repeatedly ignored their summons and imposed fines of up to $1,500 for the offense.[123]

No Flimsy Excuses

We turn now to another component of the engine that needs attention, decisions from the bench, and particularly the way judges deal with flimsy, frivolous excuses from jurors.

The Supreme Court's majority opinion in *Thiel v. Southern Pacific* (excerpted below), found the trial court had violated California Code of Civil Procedure, 201. It's a good code and should be the law of the land (my emphasis below).

> And under the state [California] law, "A juror shall not be excused by a court for slight or trivial causes, or for hardship, or for inconvenience to said juror's business, *but only when material injury or destruction to said juror's property or of property entrusted to said juror is threatened*" … Jury service is a duty as well as a privilege of citizenship; *it is a duty that cannot be shirked on a plea of inconvenience or decreased earning power.*[124]

122   Laura J. Bruch, "Ignoring Jury Duty is Now Costly," *Philadelphia Inquirer*, August 24, 2000, A1.

123   Jean Cuccione, "Jury Duty Scofflaws Get Hit in the Pocketbook," *Los Angeles Times*, August 16, 2002, B2.

124   "US Supreme Court, Thiel v. Southern Pac. Co., 328 US 217 (1946)," Findlaw.com, March 11, 1999.

I'm tired of hearing judges give great speeches about the importance and duty of jury service while weakening the pool by excusing jurors for the poorest of reasons, such as those cited in chapter 1. I'd like to see more examples of a fate similar to that of an Athens, Georgia, woman who was sentenced to two days in jail for avoiding jury service by lying about her father dying.[125]

I mentioned in chapter 1 that the voir dire process is usually conducted in open court, allowing jurors to learn what excuses will lead to dismissal. For that reason, and although it would require more court time, the process should be conducted near the bench, out of hearing range for the rest of the jury pool. Absent that, actions similar to that of a judge in Massachusetts would send a pretty strong message to the rest of the jury pool.

Judge Gary Nickerson of the Barnstable, Massachusetts, Superior Court told prospective juror Daniel Ellis, "In thirty-two years of service in courtrooms, as a prosecutor, as a defense attorney and now as a judge, I have quite frankly never confronted such a brazen situation of an individual attempting to avoid jury service." On a questionnaire the potential jurors had completed, Ellis wrote that he didn't like homosexuals and blacks.

"You say on your form that you're not a fan of homosexuals," the judge said.

"That I'm a racist," Ellis interrupted and then added, "I'm frequently found to be a liar, too. I can't really help it."

"So, are you lying to me now?" asked the judge.

"Well, I don't know. I might be," Ellis responded.

"I have the distinct impression that you're intentionally trying to avoid jury service," said Nickerson.

Ellis answered, "That's true."

Whereupon Judge Nickerson ordered Ellis taken into custody.[126]

---

125 "Dying-Father Excuse Lands Prospective Juror in Jail," *Los Angeles Times*, May 9, 2000.

126 "Jury duty excuse: I'm a racist, homophobic liar," *Associated Press*, August 1, 2007.

You recall the voir dire portion of the trial transcript offered up from the Northern California federal trial in the Flimsy Excuses section of chapter 1 and the issues I had with that judge. Compare that case with the one below. It's from a state court case I worked on in Los Angeles. The judge is the Honorable Carl J. West. I've included his name because he deserves the credit, but I've withheld the full names of the prospective jurors for their privacy.

To begin with, the judge swore the jurors in prior to voir dire. As you will read, unlike the previous example, this judge holds people accountable for their duty to the system. I have deleted some text just to move it along a little faster and to protect identities. Otherwise the transcript below is verbatim. I have picked it up at the point where the judge, having sworn in the panel before voir dire (an issue discussed in the next chapter), dealt with hardship excuses.

> Judge West: Ok, I'm going to go through hardship issues ... but we'll do it so that those of you who truly have a hardship, which is a justification for my excusing you, will not have to come back tomorrow. We try and make this as user friendly as possible; it doesn't always work. The first thing you need to know is the fact that you were cleared to come to this courtroom means that, in effect, there's a presumption that you are able to serve in this trial. Financial hardship alone may not be a justification for excusing you. Personal matters ... work-related restrictions are not necessarily a basis for excusing you for hardship. We have what is known as a one-trial one-day service program here. You come in; if you are selected to serve on a jury, you must serve for that trial. If you are not selected the one day that you are here, or, in your case, it's going to be probably two days, is the end of your service for a year. That puts demands on our system. We have about ten thousand jurors a day in the Los Angeles Superior Court system. Ten thousand a day, you can do the math. We barely have enough people in the county to bring in the number we need all the time to make our courts run. And

so you may feel that my willingness to excuse you for a hardship is kind of stingy or a little arbitrary, but you have to keep in view and keep in mind the global needs of the system; the fact that it's essential we have jurors like each one of you who bring a cross section of the community into the courthouse to decide the matters that come before the court. And those are all the apologies I can give right now. But I will certainly entertain all of the concerns that you have. So, in the front row right here, please state your name and then tell me what your hardship is.

Prospective Juror Shane: My name [is] Shane. I don't have an actual hardship or reason not to come, but just tomorrow I have a doctor's appointment. From there out, I'm okay. And the doctor appointment is about at eleven thirty.

Judge West: All right. Well, you are going to be here at eight thirty, and we'll do our best to accommodate you. If I can't, you may have to reschedule. And I realize that's a burden too, but when I have thirty-five people here, sir, I'm always going to have people with conflicts. And while I don't mean to be insensitive, and I know how long sometimes you have to wait to get an appointment, the process just doesn't work. And let me just suggest that if every time someone has a conflict we have to stop the trial and wait for somebody to take care of their personal business, we'd never get anything done. And so you have to be a little harsh at times, and I just hope that you appreciate that. Yes, ma'am?

Prospective Juror Sherilyn: My name is Sherilyn. And I am self-employed, and I'm single. And it would be difficult for twelve days [the projected length of the trial].

Judge West: What type of work do you do?

Prospective Juror Sherilyn: I'm a realtor.

Judge West: OK. Thank you. Next?
Prospective Juror Arman: I'm Arman. I'm also self-employed. I'm under contract. I'm working on measure Y for Santa Paula. It's like deadline-oriented stuff. I've got deadlines. At two o'clock today, I've got to get the brochures out. If I don't make it, they are going to sue me, and I'm going to be in a whole lot of trouble.

Judge West: You are self-employed, sir?

Prospective Juror Arman: I am self-employed, a one-man team.

Judge West: Well, the sooner I get you out of here, the better chance you have of meeting your deadline by two o'clock. Anyone else in the front row?

Prospective Juror Katherine: My name is Katherine. The only reason I'm just concerned with about staying for twelve days is on the eleventh of April I have [a] hearing for work. It's for work. It's a Cal-OSHA hearing that I have to attend to, but that's the only thing I'm really worried about is finishing.

Judge West: Okay, ma'am. Thank you. Anybody else?

Prospective Juror Nindi: My name is Nidi. I'm self-employed. I service vending machines, and I believe twelve days will be a little hard on the amount of money I'm taking.

Judge West: Okay. Thank you, sir. Anybody else in the back row?

Prospective Juror Young: My name is Young. Yesterday I told the lady I can't speak English well. I can—why I'm here now, I don't understand. My English is short.

Judge West: Okay. Sir, have you understood what I've told you so far?

Prospective Juror Young: Pardon me?

Judge West: Have you understood what I've told you so far this morning?

Prospective Juror Young: No. My house is near here.

Judge West: Okay. How long have you—what type of work do you do, sir? Do you work?

Prospective Juror Young: Yeah, I work?

Judge West: What kind of work?

Prospective Juror Young: What kind? Like UPS … courier.

Judge West: I thought you said accordion repair. And I thought that was a little unusual.

Prospective Juror Young: Many times I told the staff so they told I don't understand.

Judge West: All right. Thank you, sir. Thank you. Anyone else in the back row?

Prospective Juror Ken: My name is Ken, and I don't work for a great company. It's called (name withheld), and I'm expendable. You know, these companies, you are expendable. I'm a photographer. I take pictures of cars, and if I don't, you know, show up for maybe a week, they are going to replace me. So I could lose my job, realistically, because this company doesn't pay for nothing. I asked, "Do you pay for jury duty?" He goes, "No, we don't."

Judge West: How long have you worked for them, sir?

Prospective Juror Ken: About ten years. So, basically they say, "Hey, look, you know, you know, we might have to find somebody else. It's possible. We've got to get the job going." You know how it is?

Judge West: I understand.

Prospective Juror Ken: So, you know, I can't work twelve or however days. They might find somebody else by the time I come back. It can be gone and—

Judge West: Have a seat, sir. Thank you.

Prospective Juror Saudia: My name is Saudia. The first part is I am undergoing physical therapy right now, three days a week, which is kind of crucial to my type of employment. I'm a dance teacher. So I'm kind of at a point where it's crucial that I attend to continue my improvement. The second part is, because I'm a dance teacher, I'm kind of project-oriented toward a show. And I only see the kids and some other students once a week. So as far as twelve days, it would kind of hamper the whole deadline for my teaching them.

Judge West: Where do you teach, ma'am?

Prospective Juror Saudia: In La Canada.

Judge West: In a private school or a public school?

Prospective Juror Saudia: It's a private studio, but I also have other teaching engagements that I have with adults and so forth.

Judge West: All right. Thank you, ma'am. Anyone else?

Prospective Juror Tiffany: My name is Tiffany. It's not for sure, but there's a possibility I may have to go to New York for work on the third. I work for [name withheld], which is a fashion company. And we go into market five times a week, which is when we see the department stores and stores who buy the product, and that's next week. And I don't know today, but there's a possibility—

Judge West: Let me just say, ma'am, that work-related obligations are not the types of obligations for which I can excuse you. Your inability to attend a show or an opening or something in New York for your employer is really your employer's problem, and you have to understand that. Anyone else?

Prospective Juror Rosemary: My name is Rosemary, and the firm I work for [name withheld] only pays for ten days jury service, and I'm already on day two, so I would only have like eight more days with pay. And I have a mortgage and a lot of personal expenses and credit card bills. I don't have a husband. I'm single. And even, let's say, go to three days without my paycheck could be devastating for me because I go from check to check. I really need to get my full salary and not go beyond the eight more days that I have.

Judge West: All right, ma'am.

Prospective Juror Rosemary: Thank you.

Judge West: Let me just say, on all of these pay policies, I am more than willing to call supervisors, call your firms, and explain to them the need for you to participate if you are selected as a juror. Sometimes we worry too much about these things up front. I have thirty-five people here. We're only going to pick twelve jurors and three alternates. And so a lot of you will be gone when the process is done. But once we get down to the jury being sworn and a panel that's going to be with us, I will do everything I can to assist you so that you don't incur the hardship. And we will even try and adjust our schedule if absolutely necessary to accommodate an irreconcilable conflict. But all of that said, we still need to move forward. And jury service is really an obligation of citizenship and not something that is voluntary, as you might like to have it. So if that sounds a little heavy-handed, again, I'm always giving apologies, but we have to make the ship run here, and the only way it runs is with people like yourselves that serve as jurors. Anybody else in the front row?

Prospective Juror Rob: I'm Rob, and I know this is work-related, but I have an individual, a coworker who is going to be absent, that I am their cover for on April 10, 11, and 12. I am their sole cover, and that's my reason for requesting the excuse.

Judge West: What kind of work do you do, sir?

Prospective Juror Rob: I work for an insurance company.

Judge West: Insurance companies are regular participants in the court process. And they need to support us just as we support them every day. And so while I'm sympathetic, your company is going to have to find some way to cover this problem if you are selected as a juror in this case. Let's start left side back row.

Prospective Juror Cwenne: Hi, my name is Cwenne, and I work for a very small firm. One of our coordinators was recently called out of the office on a family emergency so I'm covering for her. And also our firm does not pay. It doesn't pay any jury duty days off. So it's a financial hardship for me as well.

Judge West: What type of work is it, ma'am?

Prospective Juror Cwenne: It's a real estate investment development company.

Judge West: The name of the firm?

Prospective Juror Cwenne: [name withheld]

Judge West: And what type of work do you do, ma'am?

Prospective Juror Cwenne: I'm a project coordinator.

Judge West: All right. Thank you. Yes, sir?

Prospective Juror Tom: My name is Tom. I employ twenty-three people. I'm involved in ongoing negotiations all the time with our suppliers and our customers. And taking me out of there for twelve days is going to be a hardship on the business. And I fear for, not myself, but my employees.

Judge West: What type of business is it?

Prospective Juror Tom: It's a radio syndication marketing production.

Judge West: Okay. Let me just explain, ladies and gentlemen, when this one-trial/one-day process came in, historically people were routinely excused from jury service without a lot of questions asked; doctors, lawyers, professionals, quite frankly, some of those people could better afford to serve as jurors and take the loss than the wage earner and the hourly employees like many of you on both ends of the spectrum here. We have tightened that up with one day/one trial. People are not excused routinely. And the burdens are substantial. And we are the first to recognize them, but it's hard to be fair when you excuse the doctor or the lawyer or the owner of a business, but you don't excuse the person who has $750 a month apartment payment and makes $8 an hour and works every day. And there really isn't a financial analysis that works in this process. I mean, we basically have to take a pretty hard line on financial reasons for not serving. And I only say that so you can appreciate where we may be going here. Anyone else in the back row? Yes, ma'am.

Prospective Juror Joan: My name is Joan H. I'm a single mom of three children, and my employer pays zero jury duty pay, but if you are willing to call them, I'm willing to stay.

Judge West: Okay. I'll certainly make the call. And there are no promises because a lot of people won't even listen to me, but I've been fairly successful in helping people that have a problem. Yes, ma'am.

Prospective Juror Jonette: My name is Jonette. I work for a very small company. I work for [name withheld]. It's family oriented. I'm the only one that's not family. There [are] only two other people in the office. My boss pays for a couple days. Even if you call, I'm going to have a hard time. He's just a jerk.

Judge West: My condolences, ma'am. How long have you worked for him?

Prospective Juror Jonette: I've worked there a little over five years. It's hard because it's close to home.

Judge West: All right. And do we have somebody else in the corner? Yes, ma'am.

Prospective Juror Gilda: I'm Gilda. I have high blood pressure, and I am on three pills. And one pill acts like a diuretic because it put me in the bathroom every now and then, just like before coming in I went to the bathroom and now I feel like going again.

Judge West: We take regular breaks. You will always have an opportunity.

Prospective Juror Gilda: And seven months ago, I fractured my left foot. And if my foot is dangling more than two hours, it gets swollen, and I find it hard to walk.

Judge West: Do you work, ma'am?

Prospective Juror Gilda: No, I'm retired.

Judge West: Okay. What kind of work did you do before you retired?

Prospective Juror Gilda: Registered nurse.

Judge West: All right. Thank you, ma'am. Back here in the corner?

Prospective Juror Lori: My name is Lori, and I'm a sales director. So basically my income is based on whether I bring in business.

Judge West: Who do you work for, ma'am?

Prospective Juror Lori: [name withheld]

Judge West: Do they have a policy?

Prospective juror Lori: They do.

Judge West: What is their jury service policy?

Prospective Juror Lori: It's three weeks, but if I don't sell then, I mean, that's pretty much what I'm employed to do is sell. And this is the selling season.

Judge West: But you are paid three weeks on a base salary basis?

Prospective Juror Lori: Yes, I get a salary, but—

Judge West: All right, ma'am.[127]

With a stipulation from the attorneys on each side, prospective juror Young, the fellow whose English was "short," was excused. The only other hardship excuses Judge West granted were Saudia, the dance teacher who was undergoing physical therapy three days a week, and Gilda, the woman with two medical conditions. He did not excuse the following:

- Shane, who had a doctor's appointment
- Sherilyn, the realtor
- Arman, the self-employed PR guy who makes brochures and was going to get sued if he didn't meet his deadline
- Katherine, the woman who had a Cal-OSHA meeting but wasn't really trying to get out of jury service

---

127　*City of Norwalk vs. Five Point U-Serve*, Los Angeles County Superior Court, 3/28/2006, case # 038298

- Nindi, the vending machine service person who probably really would have a financial hardship
- Ken, the "expendable" car photographer for a company that doesn't pay for jury service and told him he might lose his job
- Tiffany, the woman who works for a fashion company who had a trip to New York coming up
- Rosemary, the woman with only eight days left on her jury service pay and for whom the extra days without pay would have been "devastating"
- Rob, the guy covering for someone else at work, an insurance company
- Cwenne, who works for a real estate investment development company that does not pay for jury service
- Tom, who owns a company employing twenty-three people that can't survive without him
- Joan, the single mom who works for a company that doesn't pay for jury service but was willing to stay if the judge would call her employer
- Jonette, who works for a small company owned by a "jerk"
- Lori, the sales director who works on commission but also has a base salary from a company that pays for three weeks of jury service

Did Judge West seem harsh to you? Not to me. He wasn't trying to be the jury's buddy. He was always firm but polite and respectful. He was also sympathetic, but in the end, he did exactly what he had to do to make the system work, a system that he agrees is based on jury service as an obligation of citizenship.

What I particularly liked about the judge was his consistency. He said he would not excuse anyone for a financial hardship, and he didn't. His only excuses were for one man's inability to speak English well enough and for two women who had medical conditions. I also appreciated his repeated explanations of why he had to be so heavy-handed, if that's what the perception was.

If that voir dire had taken place in the courtroom of the federal judge in chapter 1 or in many other courtrooms in America, most of those people would probably have been excused, and the system would have been out all the effort and tax dollars spent summoning them.

The way it works in Judge West's courtroom is the way it's supposed to work. That said, the very real hardship situations many of those prospective jurors shared are the reasons changes need to be made in the system, changes that I propose in this book, one of the most important of which is the next one.

Jury Service Insurance

FOR THOSE WHO WOULD experience a legitimate financial hardship, there is a solution: jury service insurance. The basic concept is not entirely new. We already have a similar system in place and have had it for decades. It's called unemployment insurance, and we're all familiar with how it works. If we're working for an employer, an amount is taken from our checks each pay period for this insurance policy. The same system could be expanded to cover jury service, or a parallel plan could be implemented.

Calculating the premiums for such a policy is the ken of an actuary, but most of us know the basic principles of insurance premiums. They are based on the statistical probability an event will happen requiring payment on a policy. If the new jury pool were truly expanded to include the vast majority of our adult population, the chances of any one of us serving on a jury would be relatively slight. Accordingly, the premiums would be quite reasonable. For the self-employed, a similar plan could be designed. Just as those of us in this category must find and fund our own health plans, we would shop for the best policy for our particular needs.

The goal would be to pay jurors their full income while serving or whatever portion of that income they choose to cover. There are options for both the employee and self-employed that should be explored.

In the case of the self-employed, the previous year's tax returns or an average of the previous few years could be used to establish the limits of a full-pay option. Naturally, choosing that option would affect the premiums. In the case of an employee, responsibility for payment of the premiums would be an aspect of the employment agreement that might be open for negotiation between management and the employee or employee's union.

Many eligible for jury service would be exempt from such a plan. These would include jurors whose income is from sources that would go on paying them regardless of their status as a juror. Examples would include those on fixed incomes or incomes from trusts.

Jury service insurance should also be made available to employers. While insurance for the employee covers his or her lost wages, the employer is still stuck with the expense of a temp employee or overtime wages for the remaining employees to cover the loss of the employee serving on a jury.

Think of the effect. We would remove the most prevalent excuse from the hardship excuse list. Those excuses are almost always legitimate, even when they are offered by those citizens who would otherwise want to meet their duty. So, not only do we gain huge numbers of jurors, we improve the quality of the pool as well. Some of that improvement would result from jurors serving willingly rather than begrudgingly due to the financial hardship it causes. The system would respect them and get more respect from them.

Some version of jury service insurance should be implemented. It would even the playing field. This is the single most effective measure we can take to expand the jury pool. Indeed, I believe the pool would then balloon to its proper size, one representing a true cross section of each community.

Alternative Service

FOR MANY, THE REASON for ignoring the summons is strong enough that a fine would be preferable to serving on a jury. For that reason, a fine isn't enough. These are folks who have already shown disdain for the system and their duty. Because they are scofflaws, they are not people who should be put in a position of following the law, as a judge in a trial would give to them. I don't want to see them on a jury. Let's see, what can we do with them? What about community service? For some fixed period of time, they could work off their service. Let them pick trash side by side with those who are performing community service work as part of a judge's sentence.

Trial by Video

Getting your day in court is getting to be a lengthy battle with time. It's no secret the court systems are backlogged with cases. Delays in getting cases to trial drive up the cost of litigation. It sometimes takes years to get a court date in the more heavily used venues in America. In addition to budget cuts almost everywhere, an increase in criminal cases,[128] which have priority over civil cases, is exacerbating the problem for the civil sector.[129]

These delays have a profound effect on civil litigation and business in general. They can make it too expensive for a relatively poor plaintiff to get the justice he or she may deserve against a wealthy defendant or cause such a defendant to settle when he or she shouldn't or for amounts greater than the case is worth. They can also delay important make-or-break business decisions. "We need the resources to do both civil and criminal law," says W. Royal Furgeson, a senior federal judge in Dallas. "If decisions on contracts, mergers and intellectual property rights can't be reached through quick and prompt justice, things unravel for business."[130]

If we think of the jury pool problem as one of supply and demand, with the demands of trials exceeding the available jurors,

---

128   A 70 percent increase in the last decade

129   Gary Fields and John Emshwiller, "Criminal Case Glut Impeded Civil Suits," *Wall Street Journal* (S.F. Bay Area), November 10, 2011, A1.

130   Ibid.

then trial by video works the problem from the other end, the demand end. Video is already used to an increasing extent in trials. Witnesses are sometimes deposed[131] on videotape. Prior to the advent of inexpensive videotaping systems, a court stenographer recorded depositions only in written form. Now, many lawyers choose to videotape witnesses for various strategic reasons, including having the option of playing portions of the videotaped testimony at trial. This allows the jury to judge the demeanor of the videotaped witness, just as he or she does a live witness.

Many cases could be tried entirely in this fashion. All witnesses would be videotaped. By court order, irrelevant material would be edited out, reducing the total length of the trial, but the editing process would add an ancillary benefit. It would also cut out material, such as questions, answers, documents, and so forth, to which the court sustained an objection. This would, for example, prevent the jury from hearing improper questions from lawyers.

By contrast, the live trial system requires the judge to admonish the jury to disregard such questions. Trial lawyers know it is nearly impossible for jurors to do so. It's known as "un-ringing the bell," which can't be done. That's why trial lawyers push the limits and aren't always afraid of having a question objected to or even being admonished by a judge. They want the jury to hear something, knowing it will probably stick in their memories even if a judge tells them to ignore it.

Trial by video would eliminate this element of trial gamesmanship and improve the quality of the evidence upon which the jury decides the case. Irrelevant information would never be seen or heard. Jurors wouldn't have to be told to forget anything. The wheat would be removed from the chaff, so to speak.

Video trials need not be conducted in a courtroom. There's no need to waste that resource. They could be conducted in any number of empty classrooms in our cities. These classrooms would be empty because the trials would be conducted in the evening. This would also free up many additional jurors for duty, effectively expanding the jury pool from a different direction. Jurors would be able to

---

131   Testimony taken under oath prior to the case going to trial

continue with their jobs and fulfill various family obligations during the day. To make it easier for single-parent families, a classroom down the hall could serve as a childcare room.

This expansion of the jury pool would pick up jurors who may not have a financial hardship but whose presence at work is vital to the health of that company. This eliminates the excuses I have heard from many corporate executives, and it eliminates the virtually automatic exclusion of the self-employed.

Imagine trials conducted in local schoolrooms. There would certainly be enough room in the classrooms for more than the jurors. It would be a convenient opportunity for the public to witness a trial.

We're looking at an obligation of three to four hours a night during the week. Many, if not most, excuses for hardship would not be relevant to the video trial. This would have a downward effect on jury service insurance premiums. The school systems would receive valuable revenue from the litigants for the use of the space, and the court dockets could be cleared of backlogs.

Here's how the mechanics of the system might work. The witnesses would be videotaped under direct and cross-examination. A stenographic transcript would also be required, as it is now for all depositions. The court would rule on attorneys' objections, and the resulting witness tapes would be edited to be free of all objectionable material. There would be no need to "un-ring a bell" because the jury would never hear the "bell" in the first place.

The same procedure could be used for attorneys' opening statements and closing arguments. Again, objections are ruled on, and the opening statements are edited. Gone would be the need for judge's instructions to ignore an attorney's comments. The jury would never hear them. Again, no "bell ringing" or "un-ringing." This would put the burden on the lawyers, as it should be, to be careful about what they say. To ignore that factor would result in a chopped-up opening statement or closing argument. Not a good result for an attorney.

The entire trial would be edited before the jury is even selected. This provides an additional benefit. By being able to review the production prior to the trial, attorneys for both sides will see what the jurors will view in advance. They would be able to assess the strengths and weaknesses of their case, leading to the greater likelihood of settlement before trial. More settlements means less impact on the judicial system.

In conventional trials, attorneys aren't able to complete those assessments until after closing arguments, resulting in many trials settling during juror deliberations, after the courts' and jurors' time (that is, taxpayer dollars) have already been spent.

For practical purposes, jury selection would still be conducted using courtroom facilities if the judge were still a sitting judge. It would be impractical for a sitting judge to transport himself or herself around the county to video trial sites, and the jury pool from which the sitting jury is selected is usually around fifty to sixty people, too large for a classroom.

The manpower needed to conduct the trial would be minimal. It might include a court clerk who takes roll and plays the videotapes. A paralegal from each side could also be present to place graphic enlargements or other exhibits being referred to in opening statements and witness examinations in front of the jury. For security purposes and to maintain order, I recommend a bailiff also be present.

If a written record of the video trial were deemed necessary, a court reporter would be present. That reporter, however, should only be required to record what tapes were played, what exhibits were shown, and so forth. Easy stuff. A verbatim transcript of speech, requiring the highly skilled reporters used in live trials, would not be necessary. Lower skill level means lower cost.

The Sixth Amendment to the Constitution assures a defendant "the right ... to be confronted with the witnesses against him."[132] No problem. In a trial by video, the defendant would have the right to be present during all video depositions of witnesses, and there is no doubt he would be. His attorney would insist on it inasmuch as his attorney would need to check testimony from the witnesses against the facts his client presented to him.

---

132   Jerome Agel and Mort Greenberg, *The US Constitution for Everyone* (New York: The Berkeley Publishing Group, 1987), 42.

Trial by video would make jury service practical for many jurors who are now "hardshipped" out of the system, including reasons other than financial. It also produces a clean trial, absent information the jury should never hear but which is difficult to forget.

Night Court

This isn't new, but the concept could be expanded geographically in much the same way as with trial by video. Like video trial, it would effectively expand the jury pool by making jury service practical for those who must continue their day jobs.

This alternative requires more manpower, including the key ingredient, additional judges. This need not be a problem. Many retired judges who don't want to retire completely now serve as presiding judges in alternative dispute resolutions, like mediations and arbitrations. Arbitrations are usually binding on the parties, whereas mediations are attempts to get the parties to settle before going to trial.

Our judges come from the ranks of practicing attorneys. Many practicing attorneys are quite capable of serving in this capacity, but they may not want to make it a full-time occupation. Add to this list those attorneys who have recently retired after many years in the field but who still have the desire and ability to serve. In short, the key resources are present.

One Day, One Trial

This won't take long. It's a practice that excuses summoned jurors if they are not chosen to sit on a trial on their first day of service. It's gaining in popularity. I'm for it.

This system eliminates the waste in time and money inherent in a system that requires jurors to sit around for up to ten days cooling their heels while they wait to be seated on a jury. Frequently, that never happens, and those jurors are then excused. The one-day-one-trial system increases the burden on the court system to recruit and process more jurors, but it's a price worth paying.

In Houston municipal courts and possibly others as well, this concept has been taken a step further. The court day is split into two sessions. If a morning juror isn't chosen for a panel by noon, he or she can go home, and a new pool of jurors comes in after lunch. Jurors can have a life. They can take care of business, their children, or whatever. More jurors can serve under that system; therefore, the jury pool is expanded. As with the one-day system, the jurors also know their time isn't going to be wasted, increasing the incentive to answer the summons.

In the earlier section, Expanding the Jury Pool, I recommended dropping jurors from the recruiting lists for a number of years following jury service. Under the one-day-one-trial system, that recommendation would still hold but only for those jurors who actually serve on a jury.

Chapter 6

Impartiality and Competency

Test for Competency

Because the obligation of jury service is so important, are we justified in saying that any adult who speaks, reads, and writes English is qualified to render a decision on any issue in any trial? On the face of it, the statement makes no sense. Prospective jurors should be tested for their capacities to comprehend and reason. With an expanded jury pool, such as the recommendations in the previous chapter would produce, being more selective about who serves as jurors on each case should not create a shortage of jurors.

In support of this recommendation, I return to the Supreme Court's majority opinion in *Taylor v. Louisiana* and the excerpt I cited earlier (my emphasis below):

> In Brown v. Allen, 344 US 443, 474 (1953), the Court declared that "our duty to protect the federal constitutional rights of all does not mean we must or should impose on states our conception of the proper source of jury lists, so long as the source [419 US 522, 528] reasonably reflects

a cross-section of the population *suitable in character and intelligence for that civic duty.*"

This suggests the Court agrees that a juror should be more than just a warm body who wasn't systematically excluded from the recruiting and selection process. For some, this topic will represent another bite of forbidden fruit. They will say this is elitism. I maintain, however, that this should be one of the easiest concepts to accept.

Plenty of precedent is in our society for eligibility testing. We're tested throughout our school years, and we don't get a diploma without passing tests. Diplomas are not entitlements. We're tested even further if we want more education, in many cases before we are even admitted to a school. We don't give out driver's licenses without testing. Many jobs require testing. When we need a special medical procedure, not just any doctor will do. We go to a specialist. The list goes on. Even the army doesn't accept all volunteers. An aptitude test is administered. If you don't achieve at least the minimum score, you don't get in.

The same has even been true during military selective service years, even during times of war. An intellectual aptitude test was administered, and a minimum score was required for inductees (Forrest Gump notwithstanding). Drafting for the military is not unlike drafting for jury service. The concept of obligation or duty versus right or entitlement fits both scenarios equally. Many are called, but not all are chosen.

The evidence presented in many cases today is highly complex. In most instances, attempting to reduce the complexity of that evidence to a level comprehensible by all is futile. Good examples from my case history include patent litigation matters dealing with highly complex computer-integrated circuitry.

Conversely, the evidence in other cases is quite easy to understand with no further simplification required. A liquor store robbery case serves as a good example, where the most important evidence for the jury to evaluate is whether the witness adequately identified the perpetrator.

This suggests that a test be devised capable of determining various levels of ability. The test would be taken when the juror answers the summons. It should be one similar to those achievement tests we all had to take periodically in our school years (They were scary, but we didn't die. Bring two #2 pencils). For reasons I have already enumerated via case examples, I suggest logic ability be a significant component of the test.

A juror's test scores would translate to a rating for that individual. For the purpose of discussion, let's use a rating scale of one to five, with five being the highest level. A prospective juror's suitability to sit in judgment on a case would depend on the level achieved in the test. The juror might not be used in a case at that time, but his or her score would remain until the person was retested at a later date, if the jury pool is expanded at a much later date, if at all. Confidentiality would be extremely important. The courts should keep all test scores in the strictest confidence.

Through education and experience, people tend to gain knowledge. This suggests we should periodically retest jurors. For example, a twenty-one-year-old who tests at a level three now might achieve level four or five ten years later after schooling and other knowledge-enhancing experiences, making that individual more appropriate for complex cases.

The trial judge would rate cases on the same one to five scale. A case with a rating of one would involve evidence relatively easy to comprehend, a fender bender injury case, or perhaps that liquor store robbery example. A five would represent the highest level of difficulty, such as my patent case example. There's plenty of work to go around, so very few people would be left out completely.

An important component of the rating procedure would be input (argument) from attorneys for both sides. Each side will almost always be polarized on the issue of what level of jurors is suitable for a case. Speaking of patent cases, one in my history provides a good example.

In 1996, I worked on behalf of the plaintiff in *Loral v. Sony*. The case was unusual because, although it was tried in federal court in New York, the judge (Judge Rader) was from the Federal Circuit (the federal appeals court) in Washington DC. He had taken a special interest in the matter and gave himself the position of trial judge. It was a patent case involving the technology used in CCD chips, the light-sensing chips that replaced tubes used in TV camcorders. A win for Loral would have potentially been worth billions of dollars.

Two patents were at issue. One solved a problem called "blooming" that many of you may remember. When the camera viewed something bright, the image would "bloom," meaning the sensing device was overwhelmed with light that the CCD chip converted to electrons. The patented invention solved that problem by dumping the excess electrons in a sort of electron sewer sump. The other patent speeded up the CCD chip so it could process data faster, making for a clearer image, especially when the subject was moving (less blurring). I may have made the technology sound simple and easy to understand, but it was far from that. It took far longer for me to get a handle on it than the amount of time spent with the jury.

The technology was quite sophisticated; however, we had gone to great effort and expense to create visual materials, including computer animations, and design our case to be understood by jurors who were not technically proficient in this field. Consistent with that effort and typical of a plaintiff strategy, we wanted a jury with as many common folks as we could get. Having designed our case and our educational materials to be understood by most anyone, we wanted jurors who would rely on that evidence and their common sense in arriving at a verdict.

I say this was a typical plaintiff strategy because it was and still is. Jury research has shown that common folks are better for plaintiffs in a patent case because the defense usually has to get down into the details to persuade the jury that their product doesn't infringe. That deeper level of details is one that usually requires more education and, more than that, a different type of person who will follow you down to that deeper level. I'm not saying deeper is necessarily more relevant. It's just a fact of this type of litigation. In fact, the deeper approach may also be used to obscure the truth, which may actually be lying on the surface, so to speak.

Conversely, the defense in that case wanted jurors of the highest possible technical abilities. They argued to the judge that only jurors with these abilities would be able to understand the material and render a fair verdict. The tug-of-war during jury selection commenced.

Jury selection lasted two days. The first one went badly for us as the defense was having its way. During voir dire, the defense attorney attempted to intimidate the common folk jurors with the level of technology involved in the case, typically ending his line of questioning with one such as, "Would you be more comfortable serving as a juror in a different trial in this courthouse?" The answer from the juror was usually yes.

It was a great strategy. The defense attorney was able to get the jurors to strike themselves, so the defense didn't have to use its peremptory strikes. It also gave the jurors an easy out. By answering yes, they weren't saying they didn't want to do their civic duty. They would just be more comfortable on another case. In effect, however, they were confirming the premise of this chapter, that some jurors simply aren't competent to serve on every case and the defense's voir dire was a form of competency testing.

The jury consultant for the defense was Dr. Phil McGraw of Courtroom Sciences, a Houston-based consulting firm. We now know him as Dr. Phil, the TV psychologist. I'll assume the defense strategy was his. Anyway, it was working, and it didn't help us any that the judge seemed to favor the defense's jury profile. That first day, we lost a number of jurors who fit our desired profile, common folks without any special technical knowledge.

That evening, I recommended to lead counsel, James Wallace of Wiley, Rein & Fielding and later of BlackBerry case fame, a way to counter the defense strategy. He was to ask the prospective juror, "If the evidence is presented to you in a very simplified way and with easy-to-understand visuals, do you think you could understand it well enough to be a fair juror in this case?" In every instance, the answer was yes.

We were very successful on that second day. We ended up with a jury mostly of everyday folks, one lawyer, and one other individual with some technical training. We won the jury verdict, but Judge Rader ultimately had his way. He threw out the jury's verdict and ruled in favor of the defense, a decision that his colleagues in the

Federal Circuit later upheld. I still seethe and, furthermore, believe Rader took the case himself to assure the verdict he desired.

Fifteen years later, I attended a lawyer function that featured Rader as its speaker. I took the opportunity to ask him about that case, letting him know I had been involved. I specifically asked him why he overturned the jury verdict. His response was telling, not so much from what he said (he didn't answer the question), but the sheepish body language that accompanied the words. He said he had thought a lot about that case over the years and that his was "the toughest decision ever." Enough said. I don't believe a good and just decision troubles a judge. I also know from my client that his decision to try the case in the first place was because "the damages exceeded the gross national product of many countries" (a quote attributed to Rader by my attorney client).

Getting back on point, some cases involving highly complex materials might be tried before jurors who don't have significant technical expertise, provided the evidence is presented in a simplified form. In other matters, this might be totally impractical.

Let each side argue its position on the case rating to the judge and then live with the judge's decision and design its case accordingly. Because these decisions would be a key component in the litigation, it might be more appropriate for a panel of judges, including the trial judge, to decide case ratings.

After some experience with this procedure, the judicial system would undoubtedly settle on fixed ratings for many types of cases, eliminating the need for future ratings hearings for similar ones. However the rating procedure would also allow the judicial system to react appropriately to the demands of cases involving emerging technologies. The first trials involving a new technology may require a level five rating, whereas that rating could easily drop to a four or three with the passage of time and public familiarity with the technology.

The O. J. Simpson case might be a good example. That case relied heavily on DNA evidence, something that was relatively new to the general public, whereas many years later, the accuracy of that evidence is very well known. The case rating would be established long before the trial. Jury selection for that trial would only involve jurors with a rating equal to or higher than the case rating. That is to say, cases with a rating of one should not be decided only by jurors with that rating. The jury box for a level one case should be filled with individuals with ratings all the way up the scale. Likewise, level two cases should start with level two jurors but also include the higher levels and so on.

Within the highest levels, we might consider additional divisions according to the subject matter. For example, a case where highly complex accounting issues are key to determining a just verdict might rate a five, but a juror suitable for that particular case might not be suitable at all for another level five case involving a patent on a computer chip. So, within level five, we would need multiple divisions to account for the diversity of evidence and the suitability of jurors to judge that evidence. Only jurors who achieved the level matched to a particular case would be considered as jurors in that matter.

The danger to avoid with the juror rating system is having accounting cases, for instance, decided only by jurors with accounting degrees. (Keep in mind the dangers associated with the peers concept.) To avoid that problem, the testing and rating of jurors should not only be designed to determine what knowledge the juror has now, but what the individual is capable of learning in a trial environment. Think of it equally as both an aptitude and achievement test.

Likewise, we will always need to look for ways to teach highly technical subject matter to jurors who don't have specific training or experience in those fields. This will allow us to continue to impanel jurors with varied backgrounds, a practice relevant to the goal of achieving equity. In this context, "equity" has been defined as, "a resort to general principles of fairness and justice whenever existing law is inadequate."[133] Generally, it means the system recognizes

---

133   Michael Agnes, *Webster's New World College Dictionary*, Fourth edition (1999), 481.

there's more to deciding the fair outcome of a case than technicalities, which is why we should not dismiss the importance of commonsense reasoning.

Obviously, level five jurors will be harder to come by than jurors in the lower levels, but remember, we will expand our jury pool to include a lot of those eggheads who don't currently serve on juries. We don't have a shortage of brainpower in this country, with all evidence in our courtrooms to the contrary. We just need to include it in our jury system.

When I first suggested this concept on a TV news talk show immediately following the O. J. Simpson criminal trial, one of the panelists, an attorney, suggested this would create an elitist system, as I predicted earlier. If the definition of elite is that a juror should be able to comprehend at a high school level in order to sit in judgment on the simplest of cases, then, yes, this would be an elitist system.

That definition doesn't sound elitist to me, but that's not the point. The point is that suggesting the same juror is necessarily qualified to judge highly complex evidence is absurd. Further, to suggest that an individual who cannot even function at a minimum level is qualified to sit in judgment on any case is equally absurd.

Can we agree that some people simply lack cognitive skills? Good. Can we agree that, even among those with significant cognitive skills, no one is capable of performing in all capacities in our society? Good. This is not elitist thinking. This is common sense.

If the concept of prequalifying jurors by life experience and knowledge is elitism, then in a crude and inefficient way, we have been practicing elitism since shortly after the Boston Tea Party. Jurors suspected of having low comprehension skills are often struck by one side or another during the voir dire process. These strikes are made on suspicions, hunches, experience, and/or research. I'm sure the lawyer who made the elitist comment strikes jurors based on those same criteria when it suits his side of the case.

For that matter, when that same lawyer chooses a painter to paint his house, does he check references and licenses? Does he ask how long the painter has been in business? Of course he does. We all do, and we are testing for competency when we do so. Is the verdict of a jury less important than the verdict in the question of who paints our houses?

Assuming him to be a fine lawyer, are his clients elitist for picking him over another attorney? Are all attorneys created equal? Would it be a good idea for a divorce attorney to jump into a patent litigation case? For that matter, would it be prudent to make a junior patent attorney lead counsel in a billion-dollar case?

If testing for competency is elitism, then so is the process of creating and choosing lawyers and most other professions. Does it follow then that trial attorneys, having achieved that status through competency testing, are the most important decision-makers in a trial? Are they more important than the jury?

Sequestered Voir Dire

Earlier in this book, I identified the problem of jurors learning to get out of jury duty by observing the voir dire of those who have preceded them and copying the excuses used successfully to get out of jury service. To eliminate this dynamic, oral voir dire of individual jurors should take place outside the presence of the pool from which they are drawn. This would also improve the comfort of the potential juror by creating a more private environment for the process.

Truth or Consequences: Swear in Jurors Prior to Voir Dire

Current procedures call for jurors to be sworn in after they are empanelled—that is, after the final composition of the jury has been decided. They swear to decide the case on the evidence and to follow the law, as the judge provides. Some, but not all, jurisdictions include an oath to tell the truth prior to voir dire. This should be the law of the land.

This proposal calls for the court to prescreen all voir dire subject areas. It would be impractical to determine all the actual voir dire questions in advance because an answer to one question often leads to follow-up questions. If a juror believes he or she shouldn't have to answer questions on a particular subject or otherwise just doesn't want to, the community service option discussed earlier would kick in.

Essentially, because the Constitution calls for an impartial jury and because the courts have the right to question jurors to determine whether they are impartial, an oath to answer those questions truthfully adds a measure of assurance that the goal of impartiality is being seriously pursued. It would not provide a guarantee of success, but it would provide a measure of accountability not currently present in the system by making a violation of that oath worthy of a contempt of court citation.

Polygraph Tests: Experimenting with the Future

This will be a very large bite of forbidden fruit, I'm afraid, but here goes. This concept runs in parallel with the previous recommendation regarding the juror oath. I am proposing it as an option to that recommendation, albeit a more forceful one, for use in selected high-profile cases.

Support for both concepts is the same. First, let's revisit an excerpt from *Thiel v. Southern Pacific* offered earlier. It's from the dissenting opinion, but it is quite valuable. "Trial by jury presupposes a jury drawn from a pool broadly representative of the community as well as *impartial in a specific case*" (my emphasis).

Almost every case includes at least one issue touching on a bias of some potential jurors. Attorneys can anticipate these potential biases and ask prospective jurors whether they have one. I've seen jurors answer in the positive and be dismissed as a result. Hooray for their honesty! The search for justice and fairness, however, requires honesty from all jurors, and not all jurors are honest in that regard. They may be just embarrassed to admit a bias, or they may deny it deliberately so as to sit on a case and affect its outcome.

In all cases, the judge is the gatekeeper regarding questions put to jurors, and he or she will not allow questions in open court for all to hear that would constitute an invasion of the juror's privacy. Judges are quite strict in this regard, and I've never seen what I would consider a violation of privacy. If a juror has a concern with a question, he or she can discuss it privately with the judge. This happens all the time.

What a polygraph test would add to the process is relatively simple. Because we require jurors to be impartial in a specific case, we would be making sure they are to a much greater degree than is possible now. The court would administer the polygraph test, as well as the competency test recommended earlier, in complete confidence. Not even the prospective jurors need know the results, which, under this proposal, would be destroyed immediately after it was determined whether the juror could be considered impartial.

The courts and their polygraph experts, who would be made officers of the court, would have the exclusive right to make decisions on the subject matter and form of the questions. Those questions would be drawn from the pretrial documents with input from the attorneys.

Dr. Edward Gelb of Intercept, Inc., a Los Angeles firm, is a recognized expert in the field. According to Dr. Gelb, polygraph technology has come a long way. Computer software developed at the Johns Hopkins University Applied Physics Lab, in conjunction with specialized computer hardware by Axiton, is now used to analyze the results, which takes human judgment out of the equation.

Dr. Gelb confirms what most of us suspect: polygraph tests are not considered foolproof, even by advocates of the procedure; however, an evaluation by the United States Office of Technology Assessment showed the technology to be at least 89 percent accurate. Dr. Gelb also suggests that, with increased interest in the technology and a corresponding increase in research funds, experts could make even more improvements. Such an increase in interest and funding for improvements would certainly follow decisions by courts to incorporate the technology in our jury system.

The accuracy of the test can also be improved greatly by including multiple questions that bear on the same issue. If the results from one question are in doubt, the results on the others will clarify the matter.

We probably all know individuals who can lie with such coolness they might be able to fool a polygraph device. Perhaps they just don't have a conscience standing on their shoulder, talking into their ears and making them nervous when they lie. However, polygraph devices need not be 100 percent reliable to be a vast improvement over the current method of lie detection, which is to observe the juror answering a question and guess as to the veracity of the answer.

You may ask, "Is the system ready for such a drastic measure? It's hard enough to find jurors now. Wouldn't prospective jurors run like hell from a polygraph test?" No, the system isn't ready for it yet, at least not completely. And yes, many people would run like hell if this were a component of today's jury selection process. But for many, part of their reason for running would be that they didn't want to serve in the first place. This has been discussed at length earlier, as have the remedies, including jury service insurance to take the financial burden out of the equation. Those measures alone, however, wouldn't make polygraph tests palatable. That's why I'm recommending this as an option in high-profile cases. Our experience has shown us that many prospective jurors want to serve on these trials. They want in on the action. In such cases, truthfulness during voir dire is automatically suspect.

As Dan Sosnowski of the American Polygraph Association explained to me, analyzing polygraph results is partly objective and partly subjective. He says computer analysis has yet to arrive. In particular, he claims the algorithms used to determine what constitutes an untruthful response aren't yet reliable. A lot more testing is needed.

But we know what has been accomplished in computer sciences. Is there a faster-moving technology on earth? I have to believe that, in the not-too-distant future, computer software will be able to replace what is now the subjective component of polygraph analysis with the understanding that, for purposes of jury selection, the results needn't be 100 percent reliable. It's not too unlike our putting a man on the moon. The scientists at NASA didn't know they could do it so quickly until they heard President Kennedy tell them they were going to.

By starting with high-profile cases, we can build a history with this science in our jury system and perfect it for more extensive use in the future. In doing so, we would have to perfect not only the reliability of the science but the manner in which it is incorporated into the system. I hold to my view that jury service is a duty, not a right. As such, I don't believe the concept would need to be embraced by jurors, but only accepted.

Bear in mind that polygraph tests are already used as evidence in trials. You can't get or keep a lot of jobs without a successful result from a polygraph test. People who want those jobs don't run like hell from those tests because they are motivated to take them. In connection with their use in the jury system, obligation would supplant that motivation. As with a military service inductee, he may not like the rules, but he's in the army now.

Indulge me for a moment while I add one final rationale for what I understand is a very controversial recommendation. For decades now, jury consultants have used scientific survey techniques to reduce the guesswork in jury selection. It is not the only purpose or benefit of jury research, but it is one of the primary reasons for it.

Mock trials employ large numbers of surrogate jurors who hear very condensed versions of a case, complete a questionnaire, and deliberate to a verdict while the clients watch on video screens or from behind one-way mirrors. The questionnaires, which include extensive demographic information on the individuals as well as lifestyle data, are compared to the jurors' verdict choices. The data is then analyzed to determine the statistical likelihood of real jurors of similar demographics and with similar lifestyles coming to the same conclusion in the real trial. It's not a practice designed to discover impartiality of jurors. On the contrary, it's designed to discover biases. It is a practice that increases the odds of finding jurors who would tend to favor one side of a case. It is an expensive practice that not all parties in all cases can afford. It is also a practice known throughout the legal industry, and no rules forbid it. Implementing the polygraph recommendation would replace the science used to find biased jurors with a science useful in finding impartial ones.

Take the "Ax" Away from Attorneys

Reducing or eliminating peremptory strikes is a concept that might have been controversial a few years ago, but it seems to be getting more attention of late. Perhaps witnessing jury selection in the O. J.

Simpson criminal case, a disgraceful six-week circus, contributed to those feelings.

I'm sure the concept had been discussed long before I first heard it, but my introduction to it came from California Superior Court Judge, Burton Katz (retired). In his book, *Justice Overruled*, Judge Katz agrees with Judge Harold Rothwax, who suggests in *Guilty: The Collapse of Criminal Justice*, that peremptory strikes be limited to three.[134, 135]

Judge Rothwax reasons three strikes are needed to eliminate those jurors "about whom there is some basis for a feeling of unease."[136] He also suggests this would "undercut the rationale for 'scientific' jury consultants,"[137] which he would like to see.

For the record and as an aside, many of us refer to ourselves as trial consultants rather than jury consultants. It sounds like a small difference, but it's meant to convey that consulting with jury selection itself is a small fraction of the total assignment. Most of the work involves devising ways to explain the evidence, formulating arguments, and designing demonstrative exhibits and any number of other duties. The label "jury consultant" sticks only because that is the visible aspect of the work. That's what the courts and the public see us do.

As for what the courts and public don't see, rest assured it doesn't remotely resemble the work of Rankin Fitch, the bad guy character in the film *Runaway Jury*, or the capabilities of his organization, even though there have been times when I would have loved one of those hidden earphone gizmos. Most of the real work is too boring for a book or movie. Fitch is the product of John Grisham's fertile, if over-the-top, imagination. I know only one trial consultant whose lack of integrity mimics that of the Fitch character and who, but for a lack of intellect, might aspire to achieve such depths.

---

134   Judge Burton Katz, *Justice Overruled* (New York: Warner Books, 1997), 108.

135   Judge Harold Rothwax, *Guilty: The Collapse of Criminal Justice* (New York: Random House, 1996), 205.

136   Ibid., 207.

137   Ibid.

Though reducing the number of peremptory strikes is a step in the right direction, it's one that must be taken in conjunction with other steps, such as those I suggest. If not, we will have accomplished nothing because, together with strikes for cause, peremptories are the only way to weed out potentially unsuitable jurors. It's guesswork, but it's all we have.

Conversely, if we were to enact the various steps I recommend, the role of peremptory strikes would become moot. At that point, they could and should be discontinued altogether. The obvious example for eliminating peremptory strikes would be in cases where the jurors, in addition to having been screened for competency, had also passed a polygraph test showing no biases against either party.

I have been retained to consult on many federal cases. Those assignments usually include assisting counsel with jury selection. One case in particular exemplified the problem. It was one where the judge allowed just three peremptory strikes for each side, which, in my experience, is very typical for federal cases.

The opposition used all three of their strikes to eliminate jurors with significant education, including one who had direct relevant training and experience. In this instance, three strikes were enough to dumb down the jury. The pool was that anemic. This example also suggests that a three-strike limit will not significantly undercut the rationale for using jury consultants.

If all the recommendations I've listed were to be implemented, there would no longer be a need or justification for peremptory strikes. The jury pool would be expanded. It would more accurately represent the community. Testing would weed out those not capable of serving and would qualify the rest according to their abilities. In high-profile cases, the jurors would also be required to pass a polygraph test to determine, to a high degree of certainty, whether they were capable of being impartial in a specific case. The concepts of representation, random selection, qualifications, and fairness would have already been taken into account.

Having accomplished the above, it would be time to draw lots, fill the seats in the jury box, and let the trial begin. No lengthy oral voir dire process. No trials within trials to challenge either side's strikes. No embarrassing questions put to jurors in public, and no consultants helping to select juries, a change that would please both Judge Rothwax and myself.

CHAPTER 7

More Recommendations

Allow Jurors to Ask Questions

Commonly, jurors may ask questions of the court once they are in the deliberation process, and there is a mechanism for doing so, but although it is gaining acceptance, allowing jurors to ask questions during the trial is still rare.

Allowing questions from the jurors during trial would help prevent them from falling behind with respect to key evidence. A misunderstanding of that evidence can ripple through the juror's understanding of subsequent evidence and, indeed, the entire case. Better to try to clear up questions during the course of the trial and within the context of related testimony. No juror left behind, so to speak.

The current system expects jurors to function like computers, that is, input data, store it, process it, correlate it, analyze it, and spit out a result. That is not the way the human brain works. Allowing jurors to ask questions during the trial allows each juror to fill in whatever hole has developed in his or her understanding of the evidence so he or she can then understand subsequent information. It also stimulates greater juror involvement and investment in the process.

Many lawyers object to it because it trespasses on their territory, that is, deciding what the jurors should know in order to arrive at a verdict. This is consistent with the view of many attorneys that they are the most important people in the courtroom. They aren't. Instead, attorneys should view juror questioning as an aid to their efforts. They should want to know what jurors are thinking and what questions are lingering in their minds. Jurors will ultimately make their decision based, in part, on those thoughts anyway, regardless of the judge's instructions to the contrary, so it's best to get them out during the trial and deal with them.

According to the National Center for Jury Studies at the National Center for State Courts in Williamsburg, Virginia, as of 2005, 18 percent of state and federal trials in the previous twelve months allowed jury questions. The American Bar Association also recommends the practice.[138]

Allow Jurors to Take Notes

For those unfamiliar with the system, it may seem odd, but many courts don't allow jurors to take notes during a trial. That's sort of like a teacher telling you there's going to be a big test in a couple weeks but forbidding you from taking notes on the lectures. As I understand the arguments against taking notes, they are inaccurate notes because they are written. They have the potential to carry more weight than the memory of jurors who didn't take them.

That argument misses the mark. Note taking will always be a more accurate way of memorializing evidence than reliance on memory. I return to the mistaken notion that the human brain can perform like a computer.

If the practice of note taking is encouraged, presumably many jurors will engage in it, leading to inaccurate notes from one juror

138 Heather Won Tesoriero, Barbara Martinez, and Paul Davies, "Jurors Play Lawyer in Vioxx Case, Asking Tough Questions," *Wall Street Journal*, October 14, 2005, B1.

being challenged or corrected by the notes of other jurors, just as is the case now with jurors' memories. The more note takers, the better.

As for a note-taking juror having more influence in the deliberation room than a juror who doesn't, that basic dynamic is common in all jury deliberations, notes or no notes.

On nearly any jury, only a few in the group drive the discussion.[139] In a jury of twelve, that number is usually around four, give or take. The rest are along for the ride. The brighter, more articulate, vocal, and more opinionated jurors dominate the process. That will continue to happen whether jurors are allowed to take notes or not. Note taking will simply add a level of accuracy to the deliberation process. Someone with accurate notes will likely correct a dominant juror, for example, whose memory of the facts is inaccurate. There is no downside to taking notes.

Simplify Jury Instructions

At this writing, this is a hot topic within the legal community, though it should not be. It should actually be a no-brainer. Despite their importance, instructions by judges delivered at the close of the evidence are rendered impotent because of the complex language in which they are written. As with evidence whose presentation and language are too complex for jurors, instructions that aren't comprehended are ignored. The arrogance of the courts in persisting with this practice is counterproductive to the goal of justice, as well as indefensible and baffling. How can jurors follow laws when they don't understand them?

Beyond the comprehension issue, jury instructions are easily the most boring part of any trial. When instructions are being delivered, you can almost always find me pacing in the hallway outside the courtroom. The only reason, I'm convinced, jurors don't do likewise is that they are captive audiences. That's not to say that they aren't mentally pacing the halls of their imaginations.

---

139   I'm being conservative. In my jury research experience, it is every jury.

One might expect, if the courts want jurors to adhere to the evidence and to follow the law, they might at least make an effort at inspiring them to do so. Instead, instructions inspire daydreaming or, worse, confusion, as in the criminal trial of Richard Scrushy, CEO of HealthSouth Corp., who was accused of corporate fraud, in Birmingham, Alabama. In a note to the judge, those jurors said, "We cannot reach a verdict. We need an explanation in layman terms."[140]

To their credit, many courts are revising their instructions, and my state of California is said to be one of them. California is a pioneer in the movement to make instructions more understandable, but in a system tied to tradition, the job has not been easy. Many judges and lawyers are reluctant to make changes.

"It's almost like the Bible," said Loyola Law School professor Peter Tiersma, who sits on the Judicial Council of California. "People don't want to change a word."[141] By "people," Mr. Tiersma is referring, of course, to lawyers and judges. My belief is that they have a tendency to protect their turf. Their turf is the law, as defined by words that lawyers chooses.

Jurors in the Scrushy trial were wrestling with a thirty-six-page verdict form.[142] Nothing compared to the ninety-eight pages of legal instructions in the Michael Jackson child molestation case in Santa Barbara in 2005, including two different standards of proof for two different accusations: "a preponderance of the evidence" being required for allegations against Jackson dating back into the 1990s, while fitting that evidence into the 2005 case, which required the higher proof level "beyond a reasonable doubt." (See the scales of justice graphics in chapter 3.[143])

140   Jay Reeves, "Jurors ask judge for 'laymen terms.'" *Ventura County Star*, May 25, 2005, D2.

141   Anna Gorman, "Jurors to Face Less Legal Jargon," *Los Angeles Times*, November 15, 2004, B1.

142   Jay Reeves, "Jurors ask judge for 'laymen terms.'" *Ventura County Star*, May 25, 2005, D2.

143   Stuart Pfeifer and Henry Weinstein, "Difficult Task for Jackson Jurors," *Los Angeles Times*, June 7, 2005, A1.

The bottom line, however, is it probably makes very little difference to jurors what judges say about the evidence, at least with respect to examples like the instruction shown above. Is a judge going to be able to change the way a juror thinks about a witness's credibility via an instruction? How we each react to statements we believe are false is a very individual thing formed over a lifetime of experiences and beliefs. It is part of who we are as individuals, and no instruction is going to change that.

Allow Nonunanimous Verdicts for Federal Civil Trials

For civil cases, federal courts employ fewer jurors than state courts. Somewhere along the line, the federal courts decided that, while twelve-member juries would still be required for criminal cases, a minimum of only six would suffice in civil cases. More are usually seated to allow for the possibility of a juror or two having to be excused during the course of the trial. Federal judges usually consider the length of the trial in determining a safe number of jurors to be seated. Typical federal civil cases see juries of eight to nine.

The catch is that federal courts require unanimous verdicts for both civil and criminal cases. You remember my story of the police shooting case in Compton, California, where one juror was able to hang the jury. This practice contrasts with the practices in state courts involving a dozen jurors, where criminal cases require a unanimous verdict, but civil cases can be won by persuading nine of the twelve members. If the Compton case, for example, had a jury of twelve, even if it included two additional holdout jurors, they would not have been enough to deny a verdict in the matter.

Whatever the origin of the smaller jury size or the requirement for unanimity, I see no reason not to incorporate a twelve-member jury at the federal level and to require a consensus from at least nine in federal civil trials.

CHAPTER 8

Additional Thoughts and Parting Shots

THE JUSTICE SYSTEM HAS problems completely unrelated to jurors themselves, but which nonetheless affect their decisions. We must examine the system from top to bottom.

Judges: The Power of One

IN HIS BOOK, JUDGE Rothwax tells some very convincing war stories about bad decisions from the bench. I've also seen my share, some of which I mentioned earlier. In addition, an act of malfeasance, or at the least indiscretion, by a California judge presiding over a case I was working on prompted a report from me to the California Commission on Judicial Performance. The judge had had an affair with another trial consultant on the case, and as a favor to her, he tried to get the case transferred to his courtroom. The commission acts in relative secrecy, but I found out years later the judge in question was called in for what my source described as something of a woodshed experience. Nevertheless, he retained his position.

The table below was re-created from the website of the California Commission on Judicial Performance (cjp.ca.gov):

Disposition of Commission Cases

	2001	2002	2003	2004	2005	2006	2007	2008	2009	2010
Total Dispositions	840	901	993	1,080	954	1,023	1,058	892	1,115	1,133
Closed after Initial Review	746 (89%)	830 (92%)	906 (91%)	993 (92%)	876 (92%)	919 (90%)	975 (92%)	805 (90%)	1,007 (90%)	988 (87%)
Closed without Discipline after Investigation	66 (8%)	40 (4%)	62 (6%)	60 (6%)	51 (5%)	64 (6%)	45 (4%)	48 (5%)	74 (7%)	96 (8%)
Advisory Letter	19 (2%)	17 (2%)	16 (2%)	13 (1%)	12 (1%)	16 (2%)	20 (2%)	18 (2%)	25 (2%)	31 (3%)
Private Admonishment	5 (<1%)	6 (<1%)	2 (<1%)	8 (<1%)	6 (<1%)	7 (<1%)	9 (<1%)	7 (<1%)	3 (<1%)	8 (<1%)
Public Admonishment	0 (0%)	1 (<1%)	1 (<1%)	3 (<1%)	4 (<1%)	9 (<1%)	5 (<1%)	7 (<1%)	2 (<1%)	4 (<1%)
Public Censure	2 (<1%)	4 (<1%)	1 (<1%)	0 (0%)	2 (<1%)	4 (<1%)	1 (<1%)	0 (0%)	1 (<1%)	3 (<1%)
Removal	1 (<1%)	0 (0%)	2 (<1%)	1 (<1%)	0 (0%)	1 (<1%)	2 (<1%)	2 (<1%)	0 (0%)	0 (0%)
Judge Retired or Resigned with Proceedings Pending	1 (<1%)	3 (<1%)	3 (<1%)	3 (<1%)	4 (<1%)	3 (<1%)	1 (<1%)	5 (<1%)	3 (<1%)	3 (<1%)

The table displays ten years of statistics from the commission. You will note that, at the top of the table, total dispositions averages around one thousand cases a year and it's fairly consistent. So is the removal rate, 0 to less than 1 percent. So what does it take to get rid of a judge? What is the boundary beyond which a judge cannot step, or do cliquish winds erase that line in the sand? Are judges protecting their own, or could it simply be that judges sitting in judgment of other judges in a judicatory setting find it difficult to be judicious?

To improve the justice system, evaluating and improving the quality of our jurists has to be on our to-do list. The person with the gavel in his or her hand should be the best of the best. That is rarely the case, as the promise of much higher monetary rewards lures the sharpest attorneys to the private sector.

That fact, I would add, also contributes to a disparity in the level of talent between public sector attorneys (prosecutors and public defenders) and those in the private sector. That will not be a popular notion among public sector attorneys, but when they can convince me the whipping the O. J. Simpson prosecution team took in all aspects of that trial was just an aberration, then I'll know I'm wrong.

We need to attract talent to the public sector. That will require a reward package making the choice attractive. That should be accompanied by requiring a higher standard of talent in those positions. Ultimately, the goal should be a balanced playing field producing verdicts more as a result of facts than of the persuasive talents of attorneys. By definition, a fair trial is a trial fair to both sides.

Quality issues aside, we should be able to agree judges are as human as anyone. They weren't taken at birth and raised on special judge farms. They didn't become judges until relatively late in life, and by then, they acquired biases and internal programming just like the rest of us. They are also very powerful, and it is undisputed that power is a corrupting force. Black robes don't keep the biases in; nor do they shield the wearer from corrupting influences.

With that in mind, should we continue empowering them at current levels? I suggest not. As support for what I will recommend later, I refer back to the *Loral v. Sony* case discussed in chapter 6 and one of my now favorite targets, Judge Rader. As you recall, this was the case where the judge appointed himself as trial judge and then threw out the jury's verdict for plaintiff Loral and ruled in favor of defendant Sony.

Having read numerous briefs and expert witness reports[144] for months before the trial, I'm supposing Rader knew where he stood on the issues before the actual trial. If so, he could have saved both sides and the public a lot of money and trouble, not to mention the jurors' time, by announcing the winner much earlier. Wait! No, of course that wouldn't work. He would have simply been removed as judge, perhaps permanently, and the trial would have proceeded without him. In my litigation experience, the Loral case was an example of a biased judge who didn't get the jury verdict he wanted and threw the equivalent of a judicial tantrum.

Federal judges, like Rader, are appointed for life. We gave them that status to make them immune from outside pressures, for example, political pressures. The trade-off, however, was that we also created immunity from accountability and we gave them immense power and all that implies.

Remedy

CLEARLY THE POWER OF the bench does not go to all judges' heads, but because we can't look into their psyches, let's look for a way to hedge our bets. I'm suggesting that, if a judge wants to reverse a jury verdict,[145] he should be required to announce that intention, whereupon two other judges would read the transcript of the trial

---

144   Expert witnesses submit reports of their opinions well in advance of trial to enable the opposition to prepare their case.

145   A judge can rule in favor of either the plaintiff or defendant in a civil trial, but he or she can only overturn a guilty verdict in a criminal case.

and study the evidence. The two additional judges would not be chosen by or come from the same court as the trial judge. To reverse a jury's verdict, both of the outside judges would have to agree with the trial judge. I'll call this the "second opinion" requirement.

Furthermore, the burden of proof on the trial judge to overturn the jury verdict should be higher than the burden on the jury to make its finding in the first place.[146] Let's call it the "higher burden" requirement. The second opinion and higher burden requirements together would create a justifiably high barrier to reversing a jury decision.

Some would say the second opinion requirement is the role of the appeals courts. That is essentially correct; however, the appeals process takes years. The second opinion requirement would result in a ruling in short order. It would not replace the right of appeal, but it would send the litigants a message as to what their chances might be in the higher court. Keep in mind that we are talking about those relatively few instances when a judge overturns a jury verdict. These recommendations are intended simply to put a check on that high level of power.

That same vehicle could also be used in cases of a hung jury, eliminating the need for costly and time-consuming retrials and, in the process, making hanging a jury, for example, by an individual juror in a federal case, as with the Compton police case cited earlier, a less attractive and less powerful political statement. This, of course, would only apply to civil cases because a criminal defendant is entitled to a trial by jury.

Juries don't decide all civil trials. When the judge is also the jury, it's called a bench trial. Here the power of that one individual again comes into focus, and again I say it is too much power. I recommend a panel of three judges, with one acting as the trial judge, decide bench trials. The other two would consult with the trial judge on rulings but would otherwise only observe the trial. In this instance,

---

146 See the scales of justice explanation in chapter 3. Also, as applied to criminal cases, an increase in the burden would not be possible because the jury's burden is already at the highest level.

because there would be no jury decision to overturn, only a simple majority would be needed for a decision.

As is the case in bench trials now, the decision of the judges would be in writing, but where one judge disagreed with the other two, the dissenting opinion would also be in writing to complete the record for the appeals process.

The use of three judges is really nothing more than moving the appeals court standard to the lower courts.[147] Yes, these recommendations would increase the budget for the court system, and those costs are also easy to calculate, making them an easier target for criticism. However, we must also look at the costs of not making changes. I believe the failures of the system have cost us a great deal for a very long time and will continue to do so until changes are made. Those costs aren't as easy to calculate, but they are no less real. Additionally, referring back to issues raised in the Night Court section, the availability of retired and semiretired judges and senior attorneys would help supply the system with the additional judges needed to carry out these recommendations.

Lawyers: The Jokes Fit, You Must Admit

In keeping with the fair trial definition mentioned earlier, let's also crack down on attorneys who push the envelope to such a degree that it tear. Consider the case of the *State of California vs. Alfred Arthur Sandoval* (1985). Sandoval was tried for four murders, including killing Marlene Wells, the wife of a rival gang member in Los Angeles. The prosecutor, then-Deputy District Attorney David Milton,[148] invoked the Bible in his closing argument in support of the death penalty for Sandoval, urging the jury to do "what God says" in connection with his paraphrasing of a New Testament excerpt, "God will destroy the body to save the soul."

The jury gave Sandoval life sentences for three of the murders but the death penalty for the Wells's slaying. The death penalty verdict was appealed on the basis of Milton's use of the Bible in his closing.

---

147   Appeals courts typically use three-judge panels.

148   At this writing, he is now a Los Angeles Superior Court judge in Pomona, California.

The California Supreme Court upheld the jury verdict, calling the reference a "harmless error," but the Ninth Circuit overturned it, which meant that Sandoval would either get another life sentence for the Wells slaying or the state would have to move for a retrial on that single count.[149]

The issue here is not whether you believe in the death penalty or the Bible. It's that closing arguments should be limited to arguing the evidence in a case. The Bible was not in evidence, so the prosecutor shouldn't have used it. The prosecutor knew this when he made the argument.

Was that the only time the Bible has been used in a closing argument? Hardly. Following are the final few paragraphs of Johnnie Cochran's closing argument in the O. J. Simpson case:

> In times like these, we often turn to the Bible for some answer ... I happen to really like the Book of Proverbs. And in Proverbs, it talks a lot about false witnesses. It says that, "A false witness shall not be unpunished. And he that speaketh lies shall not escape." That meant a lot to me in this case because there was Mark Fuhrman, acting like a choir boy, making you believe he was the best witness that walked in here, generally applauded for his wonderful performance. Turns out he was the biggest liar in this courtroom during this process. But the Bible had already told us the answer, that "a false witness shall not be unpunished. And he that speaketh lies shall not escape." In that same book it tells us that a faithful witness will not lie, but a false witness will utter lies. And finally, in Proverbs, it says that, "He that speaketh truth showeth the forthrightfulness, but a false witness shows deceit." So when we're talking about truth, we're talking about truth and lies and conspiracies and cover-ups. I always think about one of my favorite poems which I think is so very appropriate in this case, you know, "When things

---

149   Henry Weinstein, "Death Verdict Voided Over Invoking of Bible," *Los Angeles Times*, November 15, 2004, B1.

are at the darkest, there is always light the next day." In your life, in all of our lives, you have the capacity to transform all Mr. Simpson's dark yesterdays into brighter tomorrows. You have that capacity. You have that power in your hands. And James Russell Lowell said it best about wrong and evil. He said that, "Truth forever on the scaffold. Wrong forever on the throne. Yet that scaffold sways the future. And beyond the dim unknown standeth God within the shadows keeping watch above his own." You walk with that every day. You carry that with you. And things will come to you. And you'll be able to reveal people who come to you in uniforms in high positions who lie and are corrupt. That's what happened in this case. And so the truth is now out. It's now up to you. We're going to pass this baton to you soon. You will do the right thing. You've made a commitment for justice. You'll do the right thing. I will someday go on to other cases no doubt, as will Ms. Clark and Mr. Darden. Judge Ito will try another case someday, I hope, but this is Mr. O. J. Simpson's one day in court. By your decision, you control his very life in your hands. Treat it carefully. Treat it fairly. Be fair. Don't be part of this continuing cover-up. Do the right thing, remembering that if it doesn't fit, you must acquit; that if these messengers have lied to you, you can't trust their message. That this has been a search for truth that no matter how bad it looks, if truth is out there on a scaffold and wrong is in here on the throne, remember that the scaffold always sways the future. And beyond the dimmer knowns standeth the same God for all people keeping watch above his own. He watches all of us, and he'll watch you in your decision and thank you for your attention. God bless you.[150]

---

150   "O. J. Simpson Civil Trial—Cochran concludes his closing statement," usatoday.com, September 28, 1995.

There is quite a bit more reliance on the Bible and references to God by Mr. Cochran than by prosecutor Milton in the Sandoval case, and it's no less inappropriate; however, the outcome was somewhat different. The state could not appeal the not guilty verdict in the Simpson case.

Where opening statements are supposed to preview, without argument, the evidence, closing arguments are also supposed to be based on the evidence but with argument from the attorney as to what that evidence means or how it should be interpreted. Is that what you see in that passage from Johnnie Cochran's closing?

Both are examples of attorneys stepping over the line and doing so knowingly. They do it in courtrooms across the country in countless ways and in countless cases. They do it because they can. They can because there is almost never a price to pay and the potential rewards are so high.

Sanctions are one way to put a price on that behavior. Sanctions should be so feared by attorneys that the risk isn't worth the reward. They take an oath and are officers of the court. They should be held to the highest standards. They are not an endangered species. Our law schools are churning them out by the thousands every year. We grant them licenses to practice their trade, just as we grant licenses to truck drivers. We demand those licenses be pulled from truck drivers who endanger the public. Attorneys who endanger the legal system should face the same fate.

The Problem with Expert Witnesses: You Get What You Pay For

Working with expert witnesses has been a focus of my practice since 1989, the year I started. And as a reminder, I'm not a lawyer. I'm a consultant. A few years later, I wrote a training booklet titled *Taking the Stand, Tips for the Expert Witness*. In the book and in seminars I conduct based on it, I teach experts how to conduct themselves when testifying in court. One of the key teachings is how to tell the truth, as they see it, under cross-examination questions designed more as lawyer testimony than actual inquiries. A guiding principle I offer on that point is that, between the witness and the attorney, only one is sworn to tell the truth. Having worked on dozens of cases over the years, nearly all of which utilized expert witnesses, it has become increasingly apparent to me that many expert witnesses don't take that oath seriously.

Jurors rely on expert testimony, as they should have a right to. Expert testimony is admitted in trials (allegedly) to assist the jury in the search for the truth. In many trials, expert testimony absolutely decides the outcome. Each side puts up its expert witness, often referred to as "dueling experts," and the side with the most persuasive expert often wins.

The ranks of expert witnesses have expanded phenomenally in direct relationship to the growth in litigation and complexity of trials. Now there are expert witnesses in every imaginable field, including forensic entomology. These are scientists who can determine when a murder took place by identifying the species of insects inhabiting the body. Gruesome? Yes, but just one example of an expertise that someone is willing to pay for.

Pay indeed! Depending on the field of expertise, the degree of competition in that field and reputation, in terms of credentials and talent, of the witness, hourly fees for these specialists can rival that of the most expensive attorneys, that is, hundreds of dollars per hour.

How can attorneys tell if they will get their money's worth, that is, testimony from the expert that's favorable to their side? In many cases, they only have to read the advertisements. Many experts market their credentials directly to either plaintiff or defense attorney groups.[151] Others work repeatedly for the same clients in the same types of cases, the proverbial hired gun.

---

151   For the uninitiated, a standard in many areas of law is for attorneys to stick solely with either the plaintiff or defense side of a case. That's how they build their reputations and market themselves. After all, they are advocates. Expert witnesses, on the other hand, are introduced to juries as "independent experts."

I have worked with many expert witnesses (no bug expert, however), and in each case, I've also seen the testimony of their counterparts. Speaking for the experts in my own file history, I can say most of them were indeed independent and honest. However, do I think their clients' interests have often affected what some experts are willing to say despite their oath to tell the truth? Yup.

I offer an example of the above from my own file history. My clients and I were working with an expert several weeks before trial. As is typical of that type of preparation work, we were putting the witness through mock examinations to see what would come out of his mouth in response to trial-like questions. This expert couldn't answer the simplest questions but wanted so much to please his client that he would give up and ask, "How do you want me to answer that?" The situation with that witness is somewhat different in that he was malleable because he was ignorant. He simply didn't know the subject matter. He was not necessarily dishonest. In any case, neither his intelligence nor his honesty was put to the test as my client did the right thing by not calling him as a witness. Would that all attorneys had that level of integrity.

Is it hard to imagine that witnesses who make a living testifying in trials would allow the wishes of the client to influence what they say on the stand, even to the extent of lying? I suspect not. You don't have to be as cynical as I am to buy into that proposition. So how is this issue dealt with currently?

The downside to lying on the stand or taking an extreme and unsupported position is that you have to face cross-examination. This process can be painful even if you are telling the truth, but there is no actual bleeding. An expert witness whose false testimony is exposed under cross-examination doesn't have to be helped off the stand, go to jail, and even get his pay docked. For that matter, it may not even cost his client the case because jurors very often don't know the difference if a lie is being told or when it is exposed.

Remedy 1: Court-Appointed Experts

We don't have to put juries in the position of choosing between two opposing experts and deciding which (if either) is giving them the straight scoop. The courts have the authority to appoint their own experts. Those experts would presumably have no motivation to favor a particular party and would have no contact with attorneys for either side (other than during examination). They would, however, be free to gather information from fact witnesses on both sides of the issue. Their fees would be part of the court costs, which are (or should be) borne by the litigants.

Think of the ramifications. The jury would be choosing which of potentially three experts to believe. Two would be poles apart, receive substantial compensation from their clients, and meet with the client's attorneys at length prior to trial. The third would not be in an advocacy role. Does that sound like a reasonably good way to assist the jury in the search for the truth? So why don't we see it on a regular basis?[152]

This practice would affect the system in at least two additional ways:

- With the presence of a court-appointed expert, some litigants might choose to forego hiring their own. They may feel that the court's expert will get the lion's share of the credibility. So why bother? That would make litigation less expensive in those cases as well as reduce the amount of court time needed to complete testimony.
- Perhaps more importantly, expert witnesses for either side would be more inclined to play it straight. The jury would be comparing their testimony with that of the court's expert, who would presumably be viewed as unbiased. For the sake of their own credibility, they would be motivated to make certain their positions were

---

152   At this writing, I've been in this business for well over twenty years and have never seen it.

well founded and would be less likely to go out on a limb for their client's sake.

The hired gun mentioned earlier who relies on repeat business from the same client or similar clients in comparable positions is motivated to be biased in his or her favor. In stark contrast, the court-appointed expert would be highly motivated to show complete objectivity to please the court and get more assignments. Presented with such an apparent imbalance in credibility, the jury's choice of whom to believe would be relatively easy. When the word gets around that hired guns will backfire in their clients' faces, that weapon could become obsolete.

Remedy 2: Peer Reviews of Expert Testimony

I mentioned earlier the absence of a downside for an expert who takes an extreme position or, in any case, a position unsupported by the relevant body of science. What I'm angling for here is a mechanism whereby those positions could receive peer review.

The idea starts with the fact that most expert witnesses belong to one professional organization or another. Doctors have the American Medical Association (AMA), electrical engineers belong to the Institute of Electrical and Electronics Engineers (IEEE), accountants join the American Institute of Certified Public Accounts (AICPA), and for the bug people, there are two groups to choose from: the American Entomological Society (AES) and the Entomological Society of America (ESA).

These entities are created in large part to establish standards within those professions and educate their members, but they also provide a stamp of credibility for those members. In the case of expert witnesses, credibility is highly prized, even essential. That's the hammer, the threat to the credibility of an expert witness through a peer review process and the creation of consequences where now there are virtually none. If expert witnesses want to go out on a limb for their clients, let there be a risk that their own professional peers will saw off that limb.

Admittedly, implementing this recommendation wouldn't be easy. It would require considerable effort on the part of those professional entities. They would have to be willing to censure their own, which is not exactly consistent with the thrust of professional organizations. However, if the threat of peer review were real enough, not only would the justice system benefit, the society itself would achieve a higher level of esteem and credibility for itself and its members.

Some variations exist within this recommendation. Professional organizations could establish the review boards connected to an adjunct membership. The adjunct membership, for an additional membership fee, would not be required of its members, many of whom have no interest in the field of litigation. Among those who do, it could still be offered as a nonmandatory membership option. Experts who don't want their trial testimony subjected to review could opt out of the plan. Sooner or later, however, they would be up against an expert who has chosen the option. Which expert is a jury more likely to find credible: the one who has avoided the possibility of peer review or the one who has been willing to risk it? A cross-examining attorney would have a field day with the former.

My preference is for a system that would require the peer review process for testifying experts, where that process is available within the appropriate professional association, with that requirement coming from the courts. This requirement would be consistent with the power the courts currently wield on this subject.

Jurors will still have to decide whom they are going to believe, but the peer review recommendation puts the credibility issue where it belongs, before the witness ever takes the stand.

Education

Finally, I offer a recommendation that the court system itself can't implement. The law, especially at it applies to juror decisions, should be taught in high school. For many jurors, high school is as far as their education goes, yet they are entrusted with extremely important decisions, ones that may well be the most important they ever make as citizens and affect all of our lives.

Certainly there are social studies teachers out there who include the law in their curricula, but I'm talking about courses dedicated to the subject. Let's make it a graduation requirement. I don't want to hear our financially strapped schools can't afford to add more classes. We've already been paying the price for not requiring this one. Perhaps they can make room in the curriculum by dumping training in self-esteem.

Lessons from Runaway Jury

I suggested in the opening statement that the many years it has taken to complete this book might have been the result of a master plan at work because those years produced so many anecdotes that found their way into the work.[153] The last of these is the film *Runaway Jury*.

When I mentioned earlier that the work of the nefarious trial consultant character Rankin Fitch doesn't resemble reality, I wasn't judging the story as a whole. Inasmuch as the story is about jury tampering, it is frighteningly close to reality. In this drama, the tampering is coming from inside the jury, which is very much in line with the nullification issue discussed much earlier, and from the outside, specifically from the defense side.

In chapter 3, I briefly mentioned the story of a juror in the O. J. Simpson criminal case who was dismissed for allegedly planning to write a book. Francine Florio-Bunten, a thirty-nine-year-old white woman and a technician at Pacific Bell, had served on the jury for five months at the time of her dismissal. An anonymous letter was sent to Judge Lance Ito, who took a dim view of jurors making book deals. An excerpt from the letter as reported by CNN follows:

> Dear Judge Ito … I work for a literary agent. I am only a receptionist … I am aware of what is happening with this office and one of your jurors … I know for a fact that my boss has entered an agreement with a juror and her husband.[154]

---

153   My wife, Donna, offered an explanation she picked up from a Deepak Chopra book about not trying to force things into happening before their time, but let's not encourage her.

154   Jim Hill, "Former O. J. juror says she was victim of jury tampering," cnn.com, April 1, 1996.

Ito began conducting interviews with the jurors to discover the identity of the offender. Juror Farran Chavarria, a twenty-nine-year-old Hispanic woman and real estate appraiser, wrote a note to Florio-Bunten about the interviews. When it was her turn to be interviewed, Florio-Bunten, not wanting to rat out her friend, denied getting the note from Chavarria and was dismissed as a result.[155] Chavarria was also dismissed shortly thereafter.

The letter turned out to be a complete hoax. No receptionist or literary agency was ever identified in connection with the letter; neither Florio-Bunten nor her husband ever came out with a book. "I wasn't writing a book; my husband wasn't writing a book. Whoever wrote that letter lied to the judge."[156] That leaves the Chavarria note issue as the only rationale for her dismissal. Why either juror was dismissed for such trivial reasons, unless you don't consider trivial Ito wanting to show everyone who was boss, is another matter.

Ultimately, the letter had the desired effect, possibly even a greater effect than planned, as two jurors were dumped for the price of one. With respect to Florio-Bunten, the apparent target of the letter, it made all the difference. In an interview with *60 Minutes* following her dismissal, she said she considered Simpson guilty and would have fought to convince the other jurors to convict.[157] "It probably would have hung the jury," she said. "I don't think I'd be able to see it any other way."[158]

As it turned out, of course, a hung jury would have been bad news for Simpson, but according to a reported interview with prosecutor Christopher Darden, if the letter's source had been investigated at the time it was received and the letter found to be fake, a mistrial

---

155   Jack Walvaren (webmaster), "The Simpson Trial Jury" from "The Simpson Trial Transcripts," law.umkc.edu (University of Missouri, Kansas City), April 13, 1996.

156   Jim Hill, "Former O. J. juror says she was victim of jury tampering," cnn.com, April 1, 1996.

157   Those would be the other jurors who practically set the record for the shortest deliberation ever.

158   Jim Hill, "Former O. J. juror says she was victim of jury tampering," cnn.com, April 1, 1996.

could have been declared.[159] That would have been worse news for the defense, as the lengthy trial would then have ended due to a shenanigan attributable to them.[160] While a retrial after a hung jury would have been a judgment call on the part of the DA's office, a mistrial would absolutely have led to a new trial and presumably one during which the prosecutors could have avoided many of their mistakes.

Jury tampering in the Simpson case wasn't as high-tech as in *Runaway Jury*, but the intent was the same. The blame for failing to investigate the letter belongs to Ito. Prosecutors Christopher Darden and Marcia Clark reportedly suspected the letter was a fraud, but Judge Ito ordered them not to examine it.[161] It was Ito's call; he blew it. But the real blame belongs to the author(s) of the letter. They were following the creed that Rankin Fitch trumpeted: "If you're relying on testimony to win this case, you've already lost it."

---

159   Ibid.

160   Does anyone doubt it came from the defense camp?

161   Jim Hill, "Former O. J. juror says she was victim of jury tampering," cnn.com, April 1, 1996.

Closing Argument

THE AUTOMOBILE, PARTICULARLY IN America, has always been an icon of freedom and our way of life. Our jury system has also been held in that light. To restore an old car that has become unreliable, do we need to look at the whole vehicle? Yes. Do we have bad laws on the books? Yes. Do we have bad judges on the bench? Yes. Do we have incompetent and overzealous prosecutors? Yes. Do we have attorneys who break the rules to benefit their clients? Yes. Many. However, under the hood of this vehicle we depend on every day, our justice system, is the jury box. The engine moves it. As with any engine, a neglectful owner pays the price in the form of breakdowns. The longer one delays necessary repairs, the more extensive and expensive they become. Making merely politically correct changes would be akin to waxing a decrepit car. Getting us back on the road with a system that has integrity, one in which we can have confidence, is now going to require more than just a tune-up.

Revisiting the major points of this book begins with a look at the present makeup of our juries. The system relies too heavily on public employees who receive their paychecks regardless of how long they serve, as well as those employers who also have generous compensation policies. The system isn't fair to those employers or the taxpayers who ultimately have to foot the bill for public employees who are absent from their jobs while serving on juries. Scofflaws and those who beg out of jury duty with flimsy excuses weaken an already frail system.

The ability of any person to serve on any case must be questioned. It makes no sense. Universal ability is not a concept we subscribe to in any other aspect of our society, let alone with respect to a component as important as our jury system. We don't hand out driver's licenses to just anyone. We require testing. You want to ride a motorcycle? That's another test. You want to drive a truck or a school bus? That's more testing. The list goes on.

Yet another test is the one jurors face after being seated in a case. The one that starts when the judge gives them instructions regarding what they must do and what they cannot do. In an automobile, all the parts have to be in working order. A defective one-dollar part can shut you down, and the jury component of the justice system is not a minor part. It is the engine itself. For the system to work, it must work as designed. It cannot neglect that duty or reinvent itself to serve a different purpose. And a duty it is, not a right.

The remedies offered in this book fit together like the steps a good machinist would take in rebuilding and engine. If you do the job right, you've got something that will prove itself reliable and long-lasting. If you cut corners, you'll be back on the side of the road with the hood up.

About the Author

DAVID TUNNO HAS BEEN a trial consultant since 1989, first with Litigation Sciences, Inc., and then forming Tunno & Associates in 1993. A frequent media commentator in connection with high-profile trials, he also authored a training manual for witnesses, *Taking the Stand, Tips for the Expert Witness*. He holds bachelor's and master's degrees from the University of Portland, Oregon, and lives in California's mother lode country with wife, Donna, where he is active in local politics and pursues a number of fiction writing projects.

Bibliography

"ACS Settles Jury Duty Lawsuit." *PR Newswire*, February 8, 1999.

"Death Penalty Thrown Out Because of Jury's Bible Study." *Los Angeles Times*, March 29, 2005.

"Declaration of Independence." Accessed December 14, 2011. www.archives.gov.

"Dying-Father Excuse Lands Prospective Juror in Jail." *Los Angeles Times*, May 9, 2000.

"Getting Out of Jury Duty is a National Pastime." *Associated Press*, July 27, 2007.

"Judge Gives Wake-Up Call." *Los Angeles Times*, April 20, 2005.

"Judge Throws out $1.5-Million Verdict." *Los Angeles Times*, November 7, 2000.

"Juror misconduct gets killer new trial." *The Record*, April 22, 2012.

"Jurors in the Robert Durst trial talk about the verdict." Accessed November 14, 2003. abclocal.go.com/ktrk/news.

"Jury duty excuse: I'm a racist, homophobic liar." *Associated Press*, August 1, 2007.

"Magna Carta, section 29." Accessed December 14, 2011. www. Archives.gov.

"O. J. Simpson Civil Trial—Cochran concludes his closing statement." Accessed December 15, 2011. www.usatoday. com.

"Tycoon Not Guilty." Accessed November 14, 2003. www. skynews.com.

"US Supreme Court, Duncan v. Louisiana, 391 US 145 (1968)." Accessed December 19, 2011. www.Findlaw.com.

"US Supreme Court, Holland v. Illinois, 493 US 474 (1990)." Accessed December 19, 2011. www.Justia.com.

"US Supreme Court, Peters v. Kiff, 407 US 493 (1972)." Accessed March 11, 1999. www.Findlaw.com.

"US Supreme Court, Taylor v. Louisiana, 419 US 522 (1975)." Accessed March 11, 1999. www.Findlaw.com.

"US Supreme Court, Thiel v. Southern Pac. Co., 328 US 217 (1946)." Accessed March 11, 1999. www.Findlaw.com.

"Woman Fired for Jury Duty, Boss in Court." *Reuters*, February 8, 1999.

"Worker Fired for Going on Jury Duty." *Associated Press*, February 8, 1999.

Agel, Jerome and Mort Greenberg. *The US Constitution for Everyone*. New York: The Berkeley Publishing Group, 1987.

Agnes, Michael. *Webster's New World College Dictionary, Fourth Edition*. 1999.

BBC Online Network. "America's Witnesses Recall Cable Car Disaster." Accessed July 25, 2003. news.bbc.co.uk.Black, Roy. Accessed March 28, 2011. www.royblack.com.

Bodaken, Edward M. and George R. Speckart. "To Down a Stealth Juror, Strike First." *The National Law Journal* 19(4) (1996).

Brainyquote.com.

Braun, Stephen. "Jury Selection Begins in First Sniper Trial." *Los Angeles Times*, October 15, 2003.

Bruch, Laura J. "Ignoring Jury Duty is Now Costly." *Philadelphia Inquirer*, August 24, 2000.

Chawkins, Steve. "Quick Pick: Jackson's Jury Chosen." *Los Angeles Times*, February 24, 2005.

City of Norwalk vs. 5 Point U-Serve. Los Angeles County Superior Court, 3/28/12, case # VC 038298, 7–19

Clark, Tony. "Marine pilot jury in 2nd day of deliberations," *Associated Press*, March 4, 1999.

Cochran and Company. Court TV, November 6, 1998.

Cohen, Joel, and Katerine A. Helm. "The Illegality of Advocating for Jury Nullification." Accessed December 10, 2011. www.Law.com.

Cuccione, Jean. "Jury Duty Scofflaws Get Hit in the Pocketbook." *Los Angeles Times*, August 16, 2002.

Decker, Twila, and Ann W. O'Neil. "Alternate Rampart Juror Complains of Panel's Conduct." *Los Angeles Times*, November 17, 2000.

Dolan, Maua. "Justices Say Jurors May Not Vote Conscience." *Los Angeles Times*, May 8, 2001.

Duane, James. "Jurors Handbook, A Citizen's Guide to Jury Duty." Accessed August 1, 2007. www.caught.net.

Elias, Paul. "Jurors on Twitter Giving Judges the Jitters." *Sacramento Bee*, March 8, 2010.

Fields, Gary, and John Emshwiller. "Criminal Case Glut Impeded Civil Suits." *Wall Street Journal* (SF Bay Area), November 10, 2011.

FIJA. "Q & A, A Primer for Prospective Jurors." Accessed July 24, 2003. www.fija.com.

Garner, Bryan A. *Black's Law Dictionary, 7th Edition*. New York: West Publishing, Co. 1999.

Gifis, Steven. *Barron's Law Dictionary, 4th Edition*. New York: Barron's Educational Series, Inc., 1966.

Gorman, Anna. "Jurors to Face Less Legal Jargon." *Los Angeles Times*, November 15, 2004.

Grisham, John. *Runaway Jury*.

Guccione, Jean. "Attorneys in Blake Trial Question Potential Jurors." *Los Angeles Times*, November 16, 2004.

Hill, Jim. "Former O. J. Juror Says She Was Victim of Jury Tampering." Accessed October 29, 2003. www.cnn.com.

Journal of the First Congress of the American Colonies, In Opposition to the Tyrannical Acts of the British Parliament, Held at New York, October 7, 1765. "Declaration of Rights." Accessed December 14, 2011. www.constitution.org.

Katz, Celeste. "New York: Your Jury May Not Look Like You." Accessed December 9, 2001. www.Nydailynews.com.

Katz, Judge Burton. *Justice Overruled*. New York: Warner Books, 1997.

Library of Congress. "Declaration of Rights and Grievances, October 14, 1774."Accessed December 14, 2011. www.loc.gov.Liu, Caitlin. "Many Pay for Doing Civic Duty." *Los Angeles Times*, July 18, 2001.

Mitsubishi Kasei Corp. v. Virgil Hedgecoth, US District Court, Northern District of California, San Jose Division, 5/23/1996, case # C-95-20800-JW, 9–11.

Overend, William. "Judge Found Not Guilty on Felony Count." *Los Angeles Times*, August 29, 2003.

Overweg, Cynthia. "Long Wait Often Goes Along with Summons." *Ventura County Star*, April 12, 2009.

———. "We Can't Pay for Jury Service." *Ventura County Star*, April 12, 2009.

PBS. "Frontline." pbs.org, 1998.

Pfeifer, Stuart, and Christine Hanley. "Radio Show Tainting Jury Pool, Ex-OC Sheriff Says." *Los Angeles Times*, April 17, 2008.

Pfeifer, Stuart, and Henry Weinstein. "Difficult Task for Jackson Jurors." *Los Angeles Times*, June 7, 2005.

Reeves, Jay. "Jurors Ask Judge for 'Laymen Terms.'" *Ventura County Star*, May 25, 2005.

Reuters. "As Jurors Go Online, US Trials Go Off Track." Accessed December 9, 2010. www.msnbc.com.

Rodriquez, Irene. "Mitsubishi Kasei Corp. v. Virgil Hedgecoth—trial transcript." May 23, 1996.

Romney, Lee, John M. Glionna, and Carol Pogash. "3 Former Oakland Officers Acquitted of Some Charges." *Los Angeles Times*, October 1, 2003.

Rothwax, Judge Harold. *Guilty: The Collapse of Criminal Justice.* New York: Random House, 1996.

Searchquotes.com.

Simon, Steven. "Is a Law Unjust? One State May Allow Juries to Decide." *Los Angeles Times*, October 30, 2002.

Stanley, Jacqueline. *Juror's Rights—Everything You Need to Know Before You Go to Jury Duty, 2nd Edition.* Naperville, IL: Sphinx Publishing, 1998.

The 'Lectic Law Library. "The Actual Facts about the McDonald's Case." www.lectlaw.com.

Van Voris, Bob. "Terra Firma Juror Dismissed After Citigroup Questions Movie Link." Accessed June 10, 2011. www. Bloomberg.com.

Vogel, Steve. "Marine Pilot Acquitted in Alps Deaths." Accessed July 25, 2003. www.Washingtonpost.com.

Walvaren, Jack. "The Simpson Trial Jury" from "The Simpson Trial Transcripts." Accessed April 13, 1996. www.law. umkc.edu.

Webster, Noah. *An American Dictionary of the English Language.*

Weinstein, Henry. "Death Verdict Voided Over Invoking of Bible." *Los Angeles Times*, November 15, 2004.

Weiser, Benjamin. "Deciding Terror Trial Location Becomes a Complex Case Itself." *New York Times*, December 26, 2009.

Williams, Scott. "Durst Jurors Speak Out: 'It Just Wasn't There.'"

Won Tesoriero, Heather, Barbara Martinez, and Paul Davies. "Jurors Play Lawyer in Vioxx Case, Asking Tough Questions." *Wall Street Journal*, October 14, 2005.

www.allpsych.com

www.quoteland.com

www.searchquotes